The Sturmgeschütz, or assault gun, served on all fronts during the war and in every campaign except the invasion of Poland in 1939. The first Sturmgeschütz units to see combat operated as independent Sturmartillerie batteries during the French Campaign of 1940 and by August of the same year they had been expanded and reorganized into battalions referred to as Sturmartillerie-Abteilungen of three batteries each.

In early 1941, the battalions were renamed Sturmgeschütz-Abteilung, although the basic organisation remained unaltered. The organisation of these units and the subsequent changes are described in the lists and charts that accompany the main text and unit histories. The armoured and infantry branches of the German Army had insufficient manpower resources to spare for the new formations and from the first they were controlled by the artillery inspectorate, as they would be until the end of the war. Their companies were therefore referred to as batteries and the artillery rank structure and titles, for example Wachtmeister, were retained.

Although the intended role of the Sturmgeschütz was to clear obstacles such as bunkers and pillboxes in support of infantry attacks, they were increasingly employed as tank killers, although ranges of less than 500 metres were essential for success. The appearance of the long-barrelled 7.5cm L/48 gun in the spring of 1942 greatly increased the anti-tank potential of the assault gun and, as the war dragged on, they issued as replacements for tank destroyers and even tanks. Significantly, the vehicles issued to Panzer and Panzerjäger formations, regardless of type or armament, were administered by the Generalinspekteur der Panzertruppen which had in fact sought control of the assault gun formations, unsuccessfully, since their inception.

As part of the mid-1943 reorganisation of the Wehrmacht's armoured units it was envisaged that the tank battalions created for the proposed nine Panzergrenadier divisions would each be allocated a Sturmgeschütz-Abteilung and at the same time the third battalions of Panzer-Regiment 24 and Panzer-Regiment 36 were converted to Panzer-Sturmgeschütz battalions, made up of two companies of assault guns and two companies of Pzkpfw IV tanks. These would be the first of the Gemischte, or mixed, tank battalions and by late 1944 the practice of maintaining at least one Abteilung of a division's Panzer regiment as a mixed battalion was common.

As with many infantry formations the Panzerjäger battalions of most Panzer divisions received a company of assault guns. The manner in which these changes affected the various branches and individual units is explained in the text.

The firm of Altmärkische Kettenwerk, usually shortened to Alkett, was the main manufacturer of the Sturmgeschütz III and was in fact the sole producer of the Sturmhaubitze 42. Founded in 1937 for the express purpose of developing and producing armoured fighting vehicles, the company was wholly owned by Rheinmetall-Borsig AG, which was itself a

Sturmgeschütz III production at one of Alkett's assembly halls in mid-1943. This photograph was taken between March 1943, when the Sturmhaubitze 42 entered production, and September when Zimmerit was introduced. The gun barrels were coated with a heat-resistant lacquer producing the dark colour evident here.

Notes

1. Reichsmarschall Göring was the minister in control of the economic expansion of Germany known as the Four Year Plan.

2. Krupp had been working on a plan for some kind of assault gun since early 1943 at least, and those designs were later incorporated into the Jagdpanzer IV programme.

subsidiary of the government-owned Reichswerke Hermann Göring (1).

The original Alkett assembly facility was located at Breitenbachstrasse 33-36 in Borsigwalde, a suburb of Berlin, and encompassed an office building and production halls which were numbered 1 to 8. By the beginning of the war the company had expanded to encompass the long-vacant Löwenberg factory at Breitenbachstrasse 1-6, on the corner of Holzhauserstrasse, which had been closed since 1928. Here Alkett built a further four production halls, numbered 9 to 12, and it was in Holzhauserstrasse that the completed armoured vehicles were actually test driven and must have been a common sight to many Berliner commuters.

By 1942 the assault gun had established its importance and Alkett had acquired most of the other buildings along Holzhauserstrasse to accommodate the growing number of administrative staff. As the war continued, other facilities were created at Breitenbachstrasse 72 and additional workshops were rented in Lichtenberg, a suburb on the eastern outskirts of Berlin, and it was here that Alkett's technical office was first established. The office and production facilities at Borsigwalde and Lichtenberg, although at opposite ends of the city, were referred to as Werke I. The company's Werke II on Eisenhammerweg, overlooking Lake Tegel about 2.5 kilometres to the north-west of the Borgiswalde plant, was known as the Maschinen und Gerätebau Tegel (MAGET) plant and eventually produced, among other weapons systems, over 400,000 MG42 machine guns.

The company's Werke III was located in Spandau between the Charlottenberg Chaussee and the Ruhlebener Altarm canal which branches of the river Spree near the Stresowstrasse bridge.

The other major manufacturer of the Sturmgeschütz III was Mühlenbau und Industrie AG (MIAG) Amme-Werke of Brunswick which began production in February 1943 with the last vehicle delivered in March 1945.

By late 1943 the Allied air offensive was gaining momentum and in November of that year, Alkett's Werke I was so badly damaged that only twenty-four vehicles left the assembly lines in December, compared to over two hundred and fifty in in the previous October. By this time the continued production of the Sturmgeschütz was essential to the German war effort and a means of resuming production as quickly as possible was discussed at a hastily convened conference attended by military and industry representatives, including a number of engineers from the firm of Friedrich Krupp. Noting that a significant number of Sturmgeschütz III superstructures had survived the bombing, Krupp's engineers proposed a simple and rather ingenious solution. Pointing out that the assault gun's superstructure and chassis were built as two separate components and later assembled in one of Alkett's factories, they suggested that the superstructure and main gun be fitted to the chassis of Krupp's Pzkpfw IV medium tank which was at that time being produced at the company's Magdeburg facility. The appeal of this plan to the Heereswaffenamt, as an almost immediate solution, is all too obvious and despite the objections raised by Alkett, the Sturmgeschütz IV was born (2).

With the exception of the prototype vehicle which was built by Daimler-Benz, Krupp was the sole manufacturer of the Sturmgeschütz IV commencing production in December 1943 and continuing until April 1945, during which time over 1,000 assault guns were built at the company's plant at Magdeburg-Buckau, with a further thirty-one converted from Pzkpfw IV tanks which had been returned to Germany for repair.

Following the December conference Alkett had concluded an arrangement with Reichsbahn-Ausbesserungswerk at Falkensee, which undertook to complete the manufacture of a number of Sturmgeschütz III chassis that could be fitted to surplus superstructures and within six months Alkett's Berlin operations had almost fully recovered. Although a devastating air raid in October 1944 succeeded in damaging most of the company's warehouses, Alkett continued to produce the Sturmgeschütz III and Sturmhaubitze 42 until the last of the assembly halls were occupied by Soviet troops during the afternoon of Monday, 23 April 1945. At least one account suggests that a number of completed vehicles left the factories that morning.

ASSAULT GUN PRODUCTION 1945

Vehicle Type	*Jan*	*Feb*	*Mar*	*Apr*	*Manufacturer*
Sturmgeschütz III	*320*	*152*	*220*	*48*	*Altmärkische Kettenwerke GmbH, Berlin (Alkett)*
Sturmhaubitze 42	*71*	*24*	*49*		*Altmärkische Kettenwerke GmbH, Berlin (Alkett)*
Sturmgeschütz III	*71*	*37*	*15*		*Mühlenbau und Industrie Amme-Werke, Braunschweig (MIAG)*
Sturmgeschütz IV	*46*	*18*	*38*	*3*	*Friedrich Krupp AG Grusonwerke, Magdeburg-Buckau*

Not included here are the older model assault guns which were sent to the factories in Germany for major repairs and subsequently returned to operational units. The records for this period are incomplete and the figure of 48 Sturmgeschütz III given for Alkett's April production is based on the numbers for the preceding months and the known quantities for total assembly.

Initially organised into six-gun batteries, the first Sturmgeschütz units saw action during the French Campaign of 1940 and were so successful that by August of the same year the batteries had been expanded into full battalions referred to as Sturmartillerie-Abteilungen. These units were composed of three batteries each and many formations retained this establishment until the end of the war. In June 1944, a number of battalions were reorganised and renamed Heeres-Sturmartillerie-Brigade and these organisational changes are described in the accompanying charts and diagrams.

The independent Sturmgeschütz units of the Heer that operated on the Western Front from the Normandy invasion until the end of the war are listed below. Although they are of course correctly described as Abteilungen or Brigaden I have used the English term battalion as a matter of convenience. As formations controlled by the artillery inspectorate, their vehicles were referred to as guns and their companies as batteries.

As the names of most of these formations were changed several times, I have endeavoured to use the official title in use in June 1944 when the campaign in the West began.

Sturmgeschütz-Abteilung 200. Formed in the summer of 1943, the battalion was renamed Sturmgeschütz-Brigade 200 in early 1944 and attached to 21.Panzer-Division. The battalion fought in Normandy, equipped with self-propelled guns mounted on the chassis of captured tanks, losing most of its equipment. Reformed and re-equipped, the battalion was attached to the Führer-Begleit-Brigade for the Ardennes Offensive, reporting that twenty-two Sturmgeschütz III and nine Sturmhaubitze 42 were on hand. When the Führer-Begleit-Brigade was upgraded to divisional status, the battalion became I.Abteilung, Panzer-Regiment 102 and served briefly in the East in February 1945 but was soon afterwards disbanded, with the remnants of the battalion forming 5.Kompanie, Panzerjäger-Abteilung 673 in February 1945.

Sturmgeschütz-Brigade 243. Formed in February 1944, after the original unit had been destroyed at Stalingrad, the battalion served in the East until August when its personnel were transferred to Altengrabow in Germany. Rebuilt with a total of nineteen Sturmgeschütz III and twelve Sturmhaubitze 42, the battalion was ordered to join Panzer-Lehr-Division for the Ardennes Offensive but was still at Altengrabow when the attack began on 16 December 1944. In fact, the battalion may not have reached the front until the last days of December at which time it was subordinated to 6.Panzerarmee, reporting that just eighteen Sturmgeschütz III assault guns were on hand (1).

In February the battalion was withdrawn from the front and in the following month was again rebuilt, also receiving a fourth Begleitgrenadier-Batterie, and was renamed Heeres-Sturmartillerie-Brigade 243. The battalion fought against the Russians in the defence of Berlin, initially without the fourth battery which took part in the defence of Westerhüsen, north of Leipzig, and joined the battalion on 21 April 1945.

Notes

1. A report of prisoner interrogations compiled by US 4th Armored Division confirms that the complete battalion was in contact with the enemy by 28 December 1944. The report also states that the battalion was equipped with eight Sturmgeschütz III and three Sturmhaubitze 42 available for immediate deployment with a further three guns in repair.

This Sturmgeschütz III ausf G displays several features that were indicative of the vehicles of 2.Batterie, Sturmgeschütz-Brigade 341 that took part in the Normandy battles including the large rain guard over the gun mantlet and the bent upper edges of the hull Schürzen. The use of fencing wire, visible here on the barrel of the 7.5cm gun, was commonly employed in Normandy as a means of holding foliage camouflage.

Photographed in the centre of Arnhem on 20 September 1944, this vehicle is one of the seven assault guns of 3.Batterie, Sturmgeschütz-Brigade 280 that took part in the defence of the city. The officer standing in the cupola is Major Kurt Kühme, the battalion commander.

Sturmgeschütz-Brigade 244. Rebuilt in March 1943 after the original battalion had been destroyed at Stalingrad the battalion was completely wiped out during the summer of 1944 in the battles around Bobriusk, south-east of Minsk in modern-day Belarus.

In October 1944 the battalion was rebuilt at Truppenübungsplatz Altengrabow, near Magdeburg in Germany, and sent to the Netherlands. In mid-December the battalion took part in the Ardennes Offensive as part of 5.Panzerarmee, reporting that fourteen Sturmgeschütz III were on hand, slightly more than a single battery. Supporting the infantry of 18.Volksgrenadier-Division, the battalion claimed to have destroyed fifty-four Allied tanks for the loss of two assault guns, although just seven were listed as serviceable at the end of December 1944.

The battalion was engaged in the defence of Cologne and ended the war fighting in the Ruhr Pocket.

Sturmgeschütz-Brigade 280. Formed in August 1943 as Sturmgeschütz-Abteilung 280, the battalion served in the East and was renamed Sturmgeschütz-Brigade on 14 February 1944. Withdrawn to Denmark after the fighting around Tarnopol, now Ternopil in modern-day Ukraine, the battalion was completely rebuilt.

When British paratroop units landed at Arnhem, Sturmgeschütz-Brigade 280 had not received its full complement of vehicles and just 3.Batterie, with the brigade commander Major Kurt Kühme, rushed to the front on 19 September 1944 with seven Sturmgeschütz III assault guns and three Sturmhaubitze 42 (1). This group remained in the area until the end of the month and Major Kühme and Oberwachtmeister Josef Mathes, the leader of the battery's second platoon, were later awarded the Ritterkreuz for their efforts in the defence of Arnhem. During the first week of October the assault guns were supporting Fallschirm-jäger-Regiment 6 near Eschen, in northern Liechtenstein, and on the first day of November 1944 received five Sturmhaubitze 42 to replace the assault guns that had been lost. The battalion fought in the battles for the Moerdijk Bridgehead and by the end of November had been transferred to Alsace where it remained until February 1945. While the assault guns were being unloaded from railway cars at Hermeskeil, south-east of Trier, they were caught in an air raid and several vehicles were destroyed.

In March 1945 the battalion received three Panzer IV/70(V) to partially offset these losses and this is the last allocation I can find for Sturmgeschütz-Brigade 280. On 26 April 1945, Hauptmann Wilhelm Lechens, who had taken command of the battalion, ordered his men to separate and make their own way home.

Sturmgeschütz-Brigade 341. Formed in early 1943, the battalion was stationed in southern France when the Normandy landings began but did not move towards the front until 25 July 1944 when it had its full complement of thirty-three Sturmgeschütz III assault guns and twelve

.... *continued on page 6*

Notes

1. Some sources give ten assault guns. At full strength the battalion would have fielded thirty-one guns and although eighteen Sturmhaubutze and twenty-two Sturmgeschütz had been shipped to the battalion prior to 19 September 1944, only a handful had arrived. The reader should be aware that allocated and received in German wartime records are two very different things.

STURMGESCHÜTZ-ABTEILUNG, JUNE 1944

All units of the German Army were organised according to instructions issued by Oberkommando des Heeres (OKH), the high command of the army. These were accompanied by detailed instructions called Kriegstärkenachweisung (KStN)which gave the authorised strength and composition of a unit listing the exact number of personnel, type of vehicle and weapons. They were not issued on a regular basis, as general orders were, but whenever an organisational change was required. Each KStN was numbered and dated, the latter being significant as some numbers were retained when an establishment was upgraded. The battalion shown here is based on KStN 416 Stab und Stabsbatterie (mot) einer Sturmgeschutzbrigade (mot) and KStN 446 Sturmgeschutzbatterie (mot) which came into force on 1 June 1944, just before the Normandy landings. Both allowed for batteries of ten or fourteen guns. The battalion depicted here is based around the ten-gun battery, or thirty-one-gun battalion, as many units were never able to carry out the reorganisation to a fourteen-gun establishment. The reasons for this are explained further in the chart on page 11.

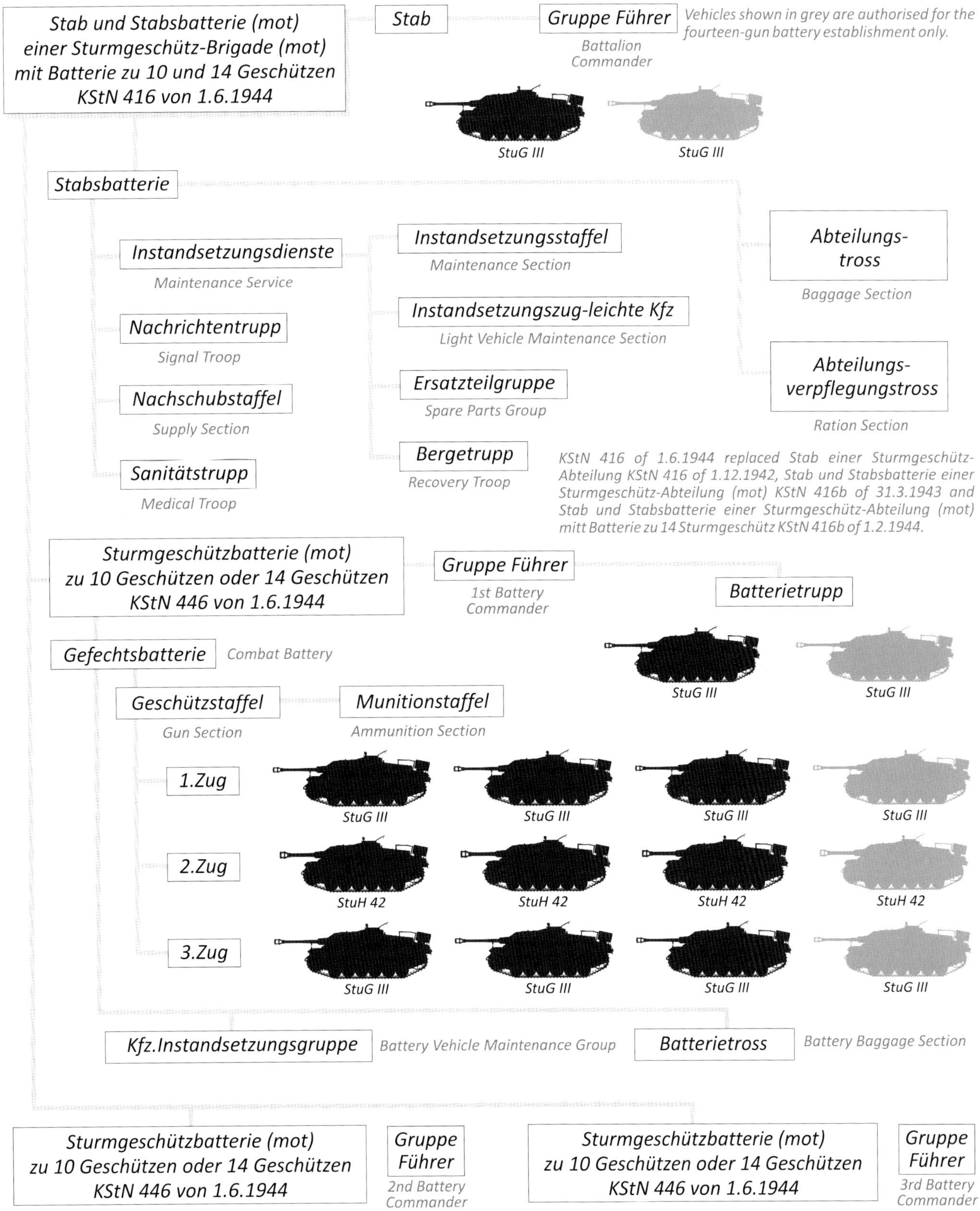

KStN 446 of 1.6.1944 replaced Sturmgeschützbatterie (mot) zu 10 Geschützen KStN 446a of 1.11.1942 and Sturmgeschützbatterie (mot) zu 14 Geschützen KStN 446b of 1.2.1944.

.... continued from page 4

Sturmhaubitze. Earlier, in May 1944, the battalion had been renamed as Heeres-Sturmartillerie-Brigade 341. The battalion suffered heavily in its first actions with 1.Batterie reporting the loss of twelve of its fourteen guns together with Hauptmann Gerd Pazur, the battery commander, Leutnant Otto Ebling, his adjutant, and Oberwachmeister Kurt Kirchner, a platoon commander and veteran of the Russian campaign. By 20 August, despite the arrival of some replacements, the battalion could report that only twenty vehicles were on hand and within five days this number was reduced to twelve. In September the battalion was withdrawn to Aachen and rebuilt and took part in the fighting in the Hürtgenwald.

In February 1945 the battalion reported that three Panzer IV/70(A) tank destroyers were on hand and these may have been the unit's last serviceable vehicles. The battalion remained in the Sauerland region into the early months of 1945 but managed to escape the Ruhr Pocket, retreating towards Kassel and the area around Magdeburg where most of the battalion surrendered to the Americans on 20 April 1945.

Sturmgeschütz-Brigade 394. Formed in May 1944 as Sturmgeschütz-Abteilung 394 for the proposed 18.Artillerie-Division, the battalion was renamed on 10 June 1944. The battalion took part in the Normandy battles, most notably at Vire in early August, and was later trapped in the Falaise Pocket. The remnants were withdrawn to Aachen and the battalion was rebuilt, reporting that twenty Sturmgeschütz III were on hand on 15 December 1944, the day before the commencement of Operation Wacht am Rhine (1). The battalion took part in the Ardennes Offensive, initially as part of 6.Panzerarmee reserve, and later under LXXIV.Armeekorps.

As part of XXXIX.Panzerkorps the battalion was engaged in the battles in Alsace and Lorraine in January 1945, reporting that twenty-three assault guns were on hand, and remained in the West when the corps was transferred to Pomerania.

In February the battalion supported 257.Volksgrenadier-Division in an assault on the Gambsheim bridgehead and it is possible that the three Panzer IV/70(A) tank destroyers received that month were used in the battle. In late March 1945, Sturmgeschütz-Brigade 394 supported 7.Fallschirmjager-Division which was opposing the Allied Rhine crossing operations near Wesel when the battalion was caught in an air raid and lost many of its remaining assault guns. Nevertheless, Sturmgeschütz-Brigade 394 continued to oppose the British advance north of Wesel and Hamminkeln, falling back through the Teutoburger Wald towards the Harz Mountains. By April the battalion had lost all its assault guns and the crews were incorporated into Infanterie-Division Ferdinand von Schill.

Sturmgeschütz-Brigade 667. Originally formed as Sturmgeschütz-Abteilung 667 in June 1942, the battalion was renamed Sturmgeschütz-Brigade 667 in February 1944 and finally Heeres-Sturmartillerie-Brigade 667 sometime in the following June.

The battalion was almost completely destroyed in the summer 1944 battles on the Eastern Front and was withdrawn to Holland and rebuilt, partly from the remnants of Sturmgeschütz-Brigade 245. In September 1944 the battalion was attached to Kampfgruppe Chill, an ad-hoc formation scraped together from elements of 85.Infanterie-Division, and may have had as many as nineteen Sturmgeschütz III assault guns and twelve Sturmhaubitze 42 on hand.

The battalion took part in the Ardennes Offensive in December 1944 as part of 6.Panzerarmee, reporting that just five assault guns were operational. In March 1945 the battalion received three Panzer IV/70(A) tank destroyers.

Sturmgeschütz-Brigade 902. Formed in January 1944 as the Lehr-Abteilung of the Sturmgeschütz-Schule West at Tours, and renamed on 14 February 1944, the battalion took part in the Normandy campaign under the direct command of LXXXIV.Armeekorps.

The battalion's initial losses were light, accounting for just three assault guns destroyed and seven crew members killed, but the battles of July would prove far more costly and by the beginning of August just three Sturmhaubitze and a single Sturmgeschütz were available for combat. In September 1944 the battalion was subordinated directly to 19.Armee and in the following October, as part of LXXXI.Armeekorps, the battalion was engaged in the fighting around Aachen reporting that seventeen Sturmgeschütz III and twelve Strumhaubitze 42 were on hand.

In early December 1944, Sturmgeschütz-Brigade 902 was attached to Korps Feldt, an ad-hoc unit of 1.Fallschirm-Armee, and later that month took part in the Ardennes Offensive as part of 6.Panzerarmee.

During the first weeks of 1945 the battalion was engaged in the defensive battles south of Bonn and by the beginning of April the first battery was near Detmold, south-east of Bielefeld, with five assault guns, while the second and third batteries were supporting 176.Volksgrenadier-Division near Brilon, almost 50 kilometres to the south-west.

Notes

1. Another report states that twenty-two Sturmgeschütz III and five Sturmhaubitze 42 were with the battalion for September and October respectively.

These two batteries were able to field eleven guns, perhaps more. All the batteries were caught in the Ruhr Pocket and by Sunday, 8 April 1945, the last Sturmgeschütz had been lost.

Sturmgeschütz-Brigade 905. Formed in December 1942 as Sturmgeschütz-Abteilung 905, the battalion was badly depleted by the battles on the Eastern Front in June 1944, and withdrawn to Germany to be rebuilt. Renamed Heeres-Sturmartillerie-Brigade 905 in the autumn of 1944, the battalion was attached to 5.Panzerarmee in the Eifel in early 1945. At that time Heeres-Sturmartillerie-Brigade 905 had twenty-two Sturmgeschütz III assault guns and nine Sturmhaubitze 42 on hand, later receiving three Panzer IV/70(A) in February 1945.

Sturmgeschütz-Brigade 911. Formed in February 1943 as Sturmgeschütz-Abteilung 911, the battalion served on the Eastern Front until August 1944 when it was withdrawn and sent to Germany. Reorganised with three assault gun batteries and a Begleitgrenadier-Batterie, and renamed Heeres-Sturmartillerie-Brigade 911, the battalion was attached to the Führer-Grenadier-Brigade during the Ardennes Offensive.

On 26 January 1945 the battalion was permanently attached to the newly formed Führer-Grenadier-Division and ended the war fighting on the Eastern Front.

Following the battles in Normandy and the subsequent retreat to the Seine, the Panzer divisions in the West were so badly depleted that in some cases they had almost ceased to exist. The remnants were gradually withdrawn from the front line and rebuilt but the shortage of tanks meant that the authorised numbers of seventy-nine Panther and eighty-one Pzkpfw IV tanks for each division could not be realised and revised organisational tables were issued for each formation.

The tank regiments of 2.Panzer-Division, 2.SS-Panzer-Division and 9.SS-Panzer-Division were made up of two battalions, each with four companies. The first battalion was designated the Panther-Abteilung and was allocated fourteen Panther tanks for each of the four companies. The regiment's second battalion was organised as a Gemischte, or mixed, Panzer-Abteilung with two companies of Pzkpfw IV tanks and two companies of Sturmgeschütze III assault guns. The 9.Panzer-Division and 116.Panzer-Division employed an identical establishment with the exception of the Gemischte Panzer-Abteilung which was made up of a single Sturmgeschütze company with fourteen vehicles.

The Panzer regiments of 21.Panzer-Division, Panzer-Lehr-Division, 1.SS-Panzer-Division, 10.SS-Panzer-Division and 12.SS-Panzer-Division were all reduced to a Panzer battalion of four companies equipped with Pzkpfw IV and Panther tanks. Of the divisions in the West, only 11.Panzer-Division was made up of two Panzer battalions of four companies each although the number of tanks in each company had been reduced to fourteen.

Those regiments equipped with Sturmgeschütz assault guns are listed on the following pages. As the history of these regiments during the Normandy battles is covered in the third book in this series, *Panther Tanks: German Army and Waffen-SS Normandy Campaign 1944*, I have not repeated those passages here.

Photographed between Aachen and Düren after the fighting in the Hürtgenwald in late 1944, this Sturmgeschütz III ausf G was manufactured between March 1944, when the later style muzzle brake seen here was adopted, and early September after which Zimmerit paste was no longer applied. Although a definitive identification of the unit to which this vehicle belongs is not possible, Sturmgeschütz-Brigade 341, Sturmgeschütz-Brigade 394 and Sturmgeschütz-Brigade 902 all operated in the area at this time as part of LXXXI.Armeekorps reserve. What may be th remains of a white-outlined number 3 is just visible of the superstructure side.

This badly-damaged Sturmgeschütz III ausf G is one of the six assault guns of II.Abteilung, Panzer-Regiment 3 of 2.Panzer-Division which attacked the town of Clervaux, in the north-east corner of Luxembourg, on the morning of 17 December 1944. Supported by infantry from one of the division's Panzergrenadier battalions, the assault guns ran into five US Army Sherman tanks and in the ensuing battle two German vehicles were knocked out. Although the Americans lost three tanks, the burning wrecks blocked the road, effectively halting any further German advance.

Panzer-Regiment 3. Attached to 2.Panzer-Division, the regiment was rebuilt after the Normandy battles with I.Abteilung made up of four Panther companies and II.Abteilung composed of two companies of Pzkpfw IV tanks and two companies of Sturmgeschütz III assault guns.

Although the authorised strength of the Sturmgeschütz companies was twenty-eight assault guns, the number seems to have never risen higher than nineteen and the twenty-four vehicles attributed to the division at the start of the Ardennes Offensive probably include those with Panzerjäger-Abteilung 38 (see below).

In March 1945, the last report prepared for the Inspekteur der Panzertruppen stated that the division had twenty-two Sturmgeschütz assault guns on hand and as other records show that the Panzer regiment's II.Abteilung could field just ten vehicles, the remainder may have been taken over from Panzerjäger-Abteilung 38. In any case, just two of the total number were considered operational (1).

According to at least one account the last three assault guns were absorbed by Panzer-Ausbildungs-Verband Thüringen (2) in April 1945 and destroyed in the fighting for Fulda. The last survivors of the division surrendered to the Americans at Plauen, near the present-day German-Czech frontier, in May 1945.

Panzer-Regiment 16. Attached to 116.Panzer-Division, the regiment was reorganised in November 1944 with I.Abteilung made up of four companies equipped with Panthers and II.Abteilung containing two companies of Pzkpfw IV tanks and one company of Sturmgeschütz III assault guns. Interestingly, a report prepared for the commander Panzertruppen West, dated 9 November 1944, states clearly that while Panzer-Regiment 16 was equipped with ten Panthers and forty-one Pzkpw IV, all the eight available assault guns were with the division's Panzerjäger-Abteilung 228.

As the Panzer regiment's I.Abteilung received a further thirty Panthers in December 1944, the last thirteen arriving two days after the commencement of the Ardennes Offensive, it may be that the companies were organised with ten tanks each in place of the authorised fourteen, with an additional tank for each battalion commander (3). This would also be correct if the eight assault guns of the Panzerjäger battalion were included in the figure of nineteen given for the Panzer regiment at the beginning of Operation Wacht am Rhein in December 1944.

During February 1945 the division was attached to 1.Fallschirmarmee and reported on 15 March that thirty-two Panthers, six Pzkpfw IV tanks and eleven assault guns were on hand, although just two of the latter were serviceable. By April 1945 the division had be so badly depleted that it was ordered to form a Kampfgruppe of fourteen Panthers and a platoon of Sturmtiger 38cm self-propelled guns (4).

Panzer-Regiment 33. Attached to 9.Panzer-Division, the regiment was rebuilt after the disastrous losses suffered in the final stages of the Normandy battles with II.Abteilung equipped with Panthers

Notes

1. The figures here are taken from Jentz. Klages' research gives the ten assault guns with II.Abteilung as Sturmgeschütz IV and also shows that Panzerjäger-Abteilung 38 was equipped with Sturmgeschütz III.
2. This Kampfgruppe was composed of some of the last remaining training units of the Ersatz Heer to be committed to front-line service and some accounts suggest that it was incorporated into the remnants of 2.Panzer-Division, not vice versa.
3. At least one authorative account gives a total of forty-one Panthers on hand during the initial stages of the Ardennes fighting as opposed to the forty we have calculated here.
4. Heinz Günther Guderian, who served as the Operations Officer of 116.Panzer-Division, mentions an action which took place in 1945 where these unusual vehicles supported the regiment's Panthers but implies that they were not actually subordinated to the division.

This Sturmgeschutz III ausf G of 2.Kompanie, Panzer-Abteilung 103 of 3.Panzergrenadier-Division was abandoned near Bastogne during the Ardennes Offensive in December 1944. The division's unit insignia can be seen at the centre of the hull rear plate to the left of the company number.

and I.Abteilung organised as a mixed battalion made up of two companies of Pzkpfw IV tanks and one company of Sturmgeschütz III assault guns.

The regiment took part in the Ardennes Offensive and the battles in the Eifel region, most notably the defence of the Erft River crossings in February when I.Abteilung reported that sixteen of its assault guns were combat-ready.

In March 1945, 9.Panzer-Division took part in the battles for the Remagen bridgehead in March 1945 by which time just fifteen armoured vehicles of all types remained. The division was trapped in the Ruhr Pocket and largely destroyed and although some elements managed to escape, it was officially disbanded on 26 April 1945. See also Panzerjäger-Abteilung 50 below.

Panzer-Abteilung 103. Raised in February 1943 for 3.Infanterie-Division (motorisiert) after the original battalion had been destroyed at Stalingrad, this formation served in Italy until August 1944 when the division was transferred to France (1). At that time the battalion contained a staff element and three companies with the third company equipped with a total of thirty-seven Sturmgeschütz III assault guns.

In October 1944 the battalion took part in the fighting around Aachen with the assault guns supported by two Pzkpfw IV tanks and a single captured M4 Sherman. In December the division was engaged in the Ardennes Offensive as part of 5.Panzerarmee, taking part in the fighting along the Elesenborn ridge, at the villages of Rocherath and Krinkelt and around Bastogne. From March 1945, 3.Panzergrenadier-Division was attached to LVIII.Panzerkorps which was attempting to destroy the American bridgehead at Remagen and reported that just four Sturmgeschütz III assault guns, six Panzer IV/70 tank destroyers and a single Pzkpfw IV tank were operational. The survivors of the division surrendered at Iserlohn, south-east of Dortmund, in April 1945.

Panzer-Abteilung 115. Attached to 15.Panzergrenadier-Division, the battalion served in Italy during 1943 and the early part of 1944. In August 1944, the division was transferred to France and took part in the battles in Lorraine where Panzer-Abteilung 115 was equipped with Pzkpfw IV tanks and Jadgpanzer IV L/48 tank destroyers. In October 1944 the battalion was reinforced by the remnants of Panzer-Brigade 113 which had been disbanded in the previous month.

The division took part in the Ardennes Offensive as part of 5.Panzerarmee, with Panzer-Abteilung 115 reporting that thirty Sturmgeschütz III assault guns were on hand in December and these may have been received earlier that month. With the conclusion of Operation Wacht am Rhein the division was moved to Holland and served there under 1.Fallschrmarmee until the end of the war.

In January 1945 the battalion took over the last Sturmgeschütz III of Panzerjäger-Abteilung 33 (see below) and in February, Panzer-Abteilung 115 had been reduced to a strength of thirteen operational assault guns and a handful of Pzkpfw IV tanks.

Notes

1. From late 1942 motorised infantry divisions were renamed as Panzergrenadier-Divisionen although the change for this unit did not take place until May 1943.

Panzer-Abteilung 2106. This battalion formed part of Gemischtes Panzer-Regiment Clausewitz in April 1945. A rather contradictory report of the same month mentions that the battalion included a Sturmgeschütz IV company with the additional notation that the vehicles were still in Dresden on 15 April 1945, at a time when the regiment's tanks were near Salzwedel over 200 kilometres away, and they are not mentioned again.

Panzer-Abteilung Putlos. Raised from the army's tank gunnery school for Panzer-Division Clausewitz, this battalion was renamed Kampfgruppe Bennigsen on 17 April 1945 and contained a single Sturmgeschütz III assault gun. Within days most of the Kampfgruppe was lost in the fighting near Fallersleben, north-east of Brunswick.

In addition to the tank regiments and battalions, the Panzergrenadier and Panzer divisions each controlled an organic anti-tank or Panzerjäger battalion that had at least one fully-armoured company equipped with assault guns or tank destroyers. Those units which operated the Sturmgeschütz in the West are listed below.

Panzerjäger-Abteilung 25. Attached to 25.Panzergrenadier-Division, the battalion was completely destroyed in the series of massive Russian offensives during the summer of 1944 (1).

Rebuilt in October with thirty-one Sturmgeschütz III assault guns the battalion fought in the Vosges region around Saarunion and Hagenau with 1.Panzerarmee.

The division took part in Operation Nordwind in January 1945 with the Panzerjäger battalion reporting that just fourteen of its assault guns were in a serviceable condition. In February 1945, 25.Panzergrenadier-Division was transferred to Heeresgruppe Weichsel fighting on the Oder Front east of Berlin.

Panzerjäger-Abteilung 33. Attached to 15.Panzergrenadier-Division, the battalion was equipped with Jagdpanzer IV L/48 tank destroyers until November 1944 when six Sturmgeschütz III assault guns were received from Panzer-Brigade 113 which had been disbanded in September after the fighting in Lorraine.

In December 1944, when the division took part in the Ardennes Offensive, the number of assault guns had been reduced to two and in January 1945 the last vehicle was handed over to Panzer-Abteilung 115 (see above).

Panzerjäger-Abteilung 38. Attached to 2.Panzer-Division, the battalion was completely destroyed in August 1944 and rebuilt in the following November with eleven Sturmgeschütz III assault guns. The battalion took part in the Ardennes Offensive and in the fighting along the Rhine and by January 1945 the number of assault guns had been reduced to seven serviceable vehicles.

In February 1945 the remnants of the battalion's personnel were transferred to the division's infantry elements.

.... *continued on page12*

Notes

1. Parts of the division were used to create Panzer-Brigade 107.

Although this photograph of a Sturmgeschütz III ausf G is of indifferent quality, it depicts several interesting features. Note the concrete armour on either side of the main gun, which appears to have been left unpainted, the factory-applied camouflage scheme in the so-called Ambush pattern, the unusually-placed Balkenkreuz and the flamboyant Sturmgeschütz-Brigade 667 unit insignia. This pattern of Zimmerit is indicative of vehicles assembled by MIAG.

HEERES-STURMARTILLERIE-BRIGADE, 1944

From early 1944, Oberkommando des Heeres (OKH) decided that all independent assault gun units would gradually be reorganised to contain forty-five guns, replacing the thirty-one-gun establishment that had been in use for almost a year. In February 1944 it was ordered that Sturmgeschütz-Abteilungen were to be renamed Heeres-Sturmgeschütz-Brigaden but this change did not alter the composition of any units and was essentially a means of differentiating the artillery's battalions from the companies of assault guns that had been raised for the Panzerjäger formations of infantry divisions. In the same month, two new organisational changes were authorised for the independent assault gun battalions which were intended to provide each with a Begleit-Grenadier battery, made up of motorised infantry, and a Begleit-Panzer battery equipped with Panzer II tanks. Subject to the availability of personnel and equipment, it was anticipated that deliveries would begin in August 1944 and all independent assault gun units would eventually contain these batteries. Although the artillery inspectorate requested that the infantry of the Begleit-Grenadier battery be carried in Sdkfz 251 halftracks, it seems unlikely, given the general shortage of vehicles at this time, that any were actually issued and there is no record of any allocation. Unfortunately no copy of the initial table of organisation, KStN 448 of 8 February 1944, seems to have survived the war and although a proposed change to the battery's establishment, which would have allowed for seventeen armoured halftracks, was put forward on 21 June 1944, this was apparently never accepted. A further version of KStN 448, dated 1 December 1944, confirms that the Begleit-Grenadier battery's transport was limited to cross-country cars and trucks. Each Begleit-Panzer battery was to have fourteen Pzkpfw II tanks but only four of these units were ever formed and all the vehicles were taken from training units and were in a very poor state. Heeres-Sturmartillerie-Brigade 667 was in fact allocated two of these units, which served as the battalion's fifth and sixth batteries, but both were lost in Russia before the battalion was transferred to the West and rebuilt in August and September 1944. In addition, the general increase from thirty-one to forty-five guns was never formalised and of the units which served in the West only Heeres-Sturmartillerie-Brigade 341 was individually authorized an increase in vehicle strength.

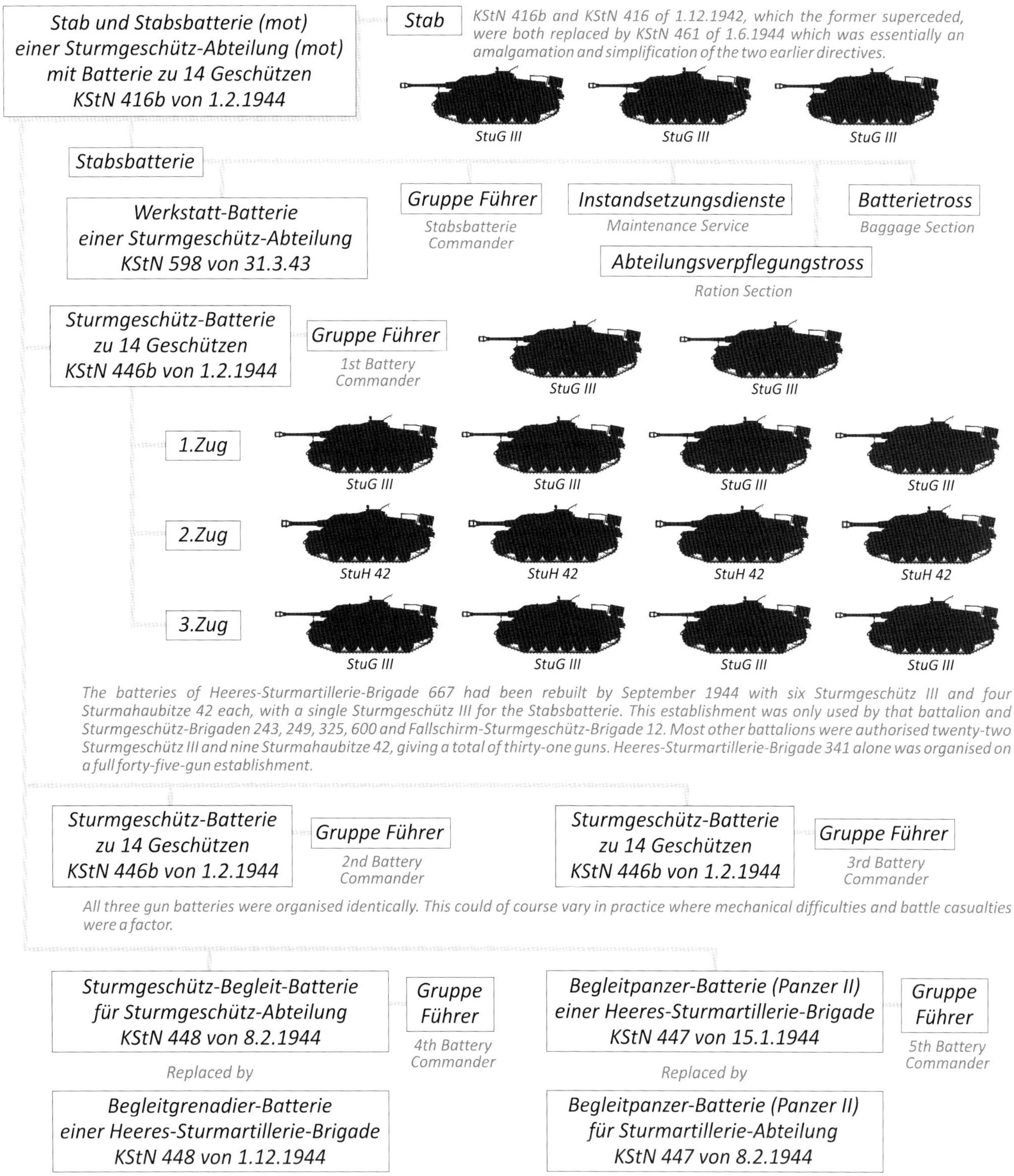

The batteries of Heeres-Sturmartillerie-Brigade 667 had been rebuilt by September 1944 with six Sturmgeschütz III and four Sturmahaubitze 42 each, with a single Sturmgeschütz III for the Stabsbatterie. This establishment was only used by that battalion and Sturmgeschütz-Brigaden 243, 249, 325, 600 and Fallschirm-Sturmgeschütz-Brigade 12. Most other battalions were authorised twenty-two Sturmgeschütz III and nine Sturmahaubitze 42, giving a total of thirty-one guns. Heeres-Sturmartillerie-Brigade 341 alone was organised on a full forty-five-gun establishment.

All three gun batteries were organised identically. This could of course vary in practice where mechanical difficulties and battle casualties were a factor.

.... continued from page 10

Panzerjäger-Abteilung 50. Attached to 9.Panzer-Division, in June 1944 the battalion was made up of a staff element, two assault gun companies and a supply company. The assault gun companies were equipped with a mixed bag of Sturmgeschütz III, Sturmhaubitze 42, Marder III self-propelled guns and Jagdpanzer IV and Panzer IV/70 (V) tank destroyers. I can offer no definitive information on how these vehicles were distributed but it is possible, although far from certain, that the Sturmgeschütz and Sturmhaubitze were allocated to the headquarters and 1.Kompanie.

On 15 March 1945 the division reported that just eight Panzer IV/70 (V) and two Sturmgeschütz III were on hand and it is likely that the latter were with Panzer-Regiment 33.

Panzerjäger-Abteilung 61. Attached to 11.Panzer-Division, the battalion arrived in France in early 1944 and was completely rebuilt. By July the battalion had eight Sturmgeschütz III assault guns, one with the headquarters, another with 1.Kompanie and six with 2.Kompanie (1).

The battalion reported in November 1944 that eight assault guns were on hand and it was at this time that the first Jagdpanzer IV tank destroyers arrived. In December the division took part in the Ardennes Offensive where Panzerjäger-Abteilung 61 operated with eight Sturmgeschütz III, which had been reduced to two by January 1945, and fourteen Jagdpanzer IV. In 1945 the division was involved in the attempts to destroy the American bridgehead at Remagen and subsequently retreated through Hesse and Thuringia into the Sudetenland where the survivors surrendered on 8 May 1945

Panzerjäger-Abteilung 228. See Panzer-Regiment 16 on page 8.

Panzerjäger-Abteilung Grossdeutscland. Ordered to join Panzer-Division Clausewitz in early April 1945, the battalion lost all its new Panzer IV/70(V) tank destroyers during the fighting in East Prussia before the transfer could take place and had to be refitted with Sturmgeschütz III assault guns.

Formed from two companies of the Grossdeutschland division and one company from Panzer-Abteilung Potsdam, at one time the battalion had a motorised Begleit-Kompanie attached to the headquarters. On 6 April 1945 the battalion reported that thirty-one assault guns were on hand.

From late July 1944 the Oberkommando des Heeres (OKH), at the insistence of Hitler, raised a number of independent Panzer brigades. Although strong in armour they lacked the support elements of the Panzer divisions, most crucially the artillery assets, and most had been either destroyed or disbanded by the end of the year.

Numbered from 101 to 113, the first ten brigades each contained a Panzer battalion while the last three were formed with the equivalent of a full regiment. Both types were allocated an assault gun

Notes

1. The companies were also equipped with the Panzerjäger II für 7,5 cm Pak 40/2, more commonly referred to as Marder II, and Panzerjäger 38 t für 7,62 cm Pak 36, or Marder III. As a matter of interest, the third company was armed with towed 7.5cm Pak 40 guns.

Abandoned on the outskirts of Mölsheim, west of Worms, in March 1945, the hull Schürzen of this Sturmgeschütz III ausf G have been removed and placed in front of the vehicle, probably as extra armour protection. The company number of 023 would suggest a vehicle of an anti-tank unit and although a positive identification is not possible, Panzerjäger-Abteilung 1559, which reported that a number of theses vehicles were on hand, was in the area at this time. Note the metal plate bolted over the hole for the Rundumsfeuer remote-control machine gun.

The caption of this US Army Signal Corps photograph states that it was taken in February 1945 after the surrender of the German units defending the area around Haus Rath at Düren, south-west of Cologne. General Courtney Hodges, who commanded the US 1st Army, mentions what he refers to as Panzergrenadier division in his account of the fighting here but I have been unable to find any record of a unit equipped with Sturmgeschütz III assault guns. Neither the US Army or OKW situation maps for this period show any units equipped with these vehicles in the area. Note the stylised mouth and eyes painted onto the Topfblende gun mantlet.

company, referred to as the Panzerjäger (Sturmgeschütz) Kompanie. The organisations varied and even official contemporary accounts are quite confusing. A complete and full analysis of these formations is far beyond the scope of this book and may be the subject of a future title.

Those units which served in the West and were equipped with Sturmgeschütz III assault guns are listed below.

Sturmgeschütz-Kompanie 2111. Attached to Panzer-Brigade 111, the battalion reported that ten assault guns were on hand in September 1944. There is some debate over whether these vehicles were Sturmgeschütz III or Jagdpanzer IV tank destroyers with which a number of the earlier brigades were equipped.

The brigade was essentially destroyed as a fighting force in the battles around Luneville and Arracourt in late September 1944.

Sturmgeschütz-Kompanie 2112. Attached to Panzer-Brigade 112, the battalion was equipped with ten Sturmgeschütz III assault guns in September 1944. The brigade suffered heavily in the fighting in Lorraine in mid-September, losing thirty-seven Panthers and twenty-three Pzkpfw IV tanks in a single day, and was disbanded later that month.

Sturmgeschütz-Kompanie 2113. Attached to Panzer-Brigade 113, the battalion contained ten Sturmgeschütz III assault guns. The brigade was badly depleted in the battles in Lorraine in September 1944 and disbanded, the survivors going to Panzer-Abteilung 115.

In early 1944, while the first heavy Panzerjäger units equipped with the Jagdpanther tank destroyer were being formed, Hitler directed that a new organisation be trialled where the battalions would be made up of a single company of Jagdpanthers and two companies of Sturmgeschütz III assault guns. Of the units that served on the Western Front just two were affected by this order and they are shown below.

As these battalions are covered in some detail in *Jagdpanther Tank Destroyer: German Army and Waffen-SS Western Europe 1944-1945*, the eighth book in this series, I will mention them only briefly here.

Schwere Panzerjäger-Abteilung 519. The battalion served on the Russian Front until July 1944 when it was withdrawn to Truppenübungsplatz Mielau in Germany to be rebuilt.

Renamed schwere Panzerjäger-Abteilung 519 (Panther) on 15 September 1944, the battalion was organised with a Stabskompanie of three Jagdpanthers, 1.Kompanie with fourteen Jagdpanthers and the second and third companies with fourteen Sturmgeschütz III assault guns each. The Jagdpanthers were sent into action almost immediately, supporting I.SS-Panzerkorps and 116.Panzer-Division in the battles for the Hürtgen Forest. From 29 November 1944, the

.... continued on page15

SCHWERE PANZERJÄGER-ABTEILUNG, SEPTEMBER 1944

The initial organisation of a Jagdpanther battalion, or schwere Panzerjäger-Abteilung (Panther), called for a Stab, or headquarters, with three Jagdpanthers and a Stabskompanie made up of a signals platoon (Nachrichten-Zug), an armoured engineer platoon (Pionier-Zug) and an anti-aircraft defence platoon (Fliegerabwehr-Zug). Due to a shortage of suitable vehicles, and Hitler's insistence that these units be rushed into service as soon as possible, in September 1944 a new organisation was introduced where only the first company was to be equipped with Jagdpanthers while the second and third companies were outfitted with Sturmgeschütz III assault guns, and later with Jagdpanzer IV tank destroyers. In his post-war memoirs Oberleutnant Franz Kopka, who served as a company commander with schwere Panzerjäger-Abteilung 559, also mentions a medical platoon or Sanitäts-Zug and I have included that here.

Stab, schwere Panzerjäger-Abteilung 'Panther' (frei Gliederung) KStN 1106a (fG) von 1.3.1944.

Panzerjägerbefehlswagen equipped with Funkgerät (FuG) 8 and FuG5 radios

Jagdpanther equipped with FuG7 and FuG5 radios

Stabskompanie einer schweren Panzerjäger-Abteilung 'Panther' (frei Gliederung) KStN 1154a (fG) von 1.3.1944.

- Nachrichten-Zug: 1 x Sdkfz 251
- Pionier-Zug: 4 x Sdkfz 251
- Fliegerabwehr-Zug: 3 x FlakPz IV 2cm
- Sanitäts-Zug: 2 x Sdkfz 251

The expression 'frei Gliederung' refers to the concept of free organisation which was introduced in early 1944 where certain support elements, such as transport or supply, were removed from companies and held at battalion or regimental level.

Versorgungs-Kompanie einer schwere Panzerjäger-Abteilung 'Panther' (frei Gliederung) KStN 1163a (fG) von 1.3.1944.

Schwere Panzerjäger-Kompanie 'Panther' (frei Gliederung) KStN 1149a (fG) von 1.3.1944.

Each company commander's vehicle was equipped with an FuG8 and FuG5 radio while the four platoon commanders had FuG5 and FuG2 sets. The remaining vehicles were fitted with a single FuG5 radio.

- Gruppe Führer (1st Company Commander): Jagdpanther, Jagdpanther
- 1.Zug: Jagdpanther, Jagdpanther, Jagdpanther, Jagdpanther
- 2.Zug: Jagdpanther, Jagdpanther, Jagdpanther, Jagdpanther
- 3.Zug: Jagdpanther, Jagdpanther, Jagdpanther, Jagdpanther

The FuG8 radio set was fitted to command vehicles and had an operating range of 25 kilometres to 140 kilometres, although the vehicle needed to be stationary and fitted with a special antenna to achieve the latter. In tanks it could be identified by the distinctive Sternantenna D, or star antenna. The FuG7 set had a range of between 60 and 80 kilometres and was mostly used to communicate with ground-attack aircraft although by late 1944 the opportunities for this were rare. The FuG5 was the standard radio for tank-to-tank communication at platoon and company level and had a maximum range of 4 kilometres. The FuG2 was an additional receiver that allowed platoon commanders to monitor battalion or regimental frequencies while simultaneously communicating with the tanks under their command.

Panzerjäger-Sturmgeschütz-Kompanie (frei Gliederung) KStN 1149 (fG) von 1.4.1944.

- Gruppe Führer (2nd Company Commander): StuG III, StuG III
- 1.Zug: StuG III, StuG III, StuG III, StuG III
- 2.Zug: StuG III, StuG III, StuG III, StuG III
- 3.Zug: StuG III, StuG III, StuG III, StuG III

Panzerjäger-Sturmgeschütz-Kompanie (frei Gliederung) KStN 1149 (fG) von 1.4.1944.

- Gruppe Führer (3rd Company Commander)
- 1.Zug
- 2.Zug
- 3.Zug

.... *continued from page 13*

battalion was engaged at Lucherberg, north-west of Düren in western Germany, in support of Panzer-Abteilung (Funklenk) 301. During these actions the battalion was able to report that ten Jagdpanthers and twenty-two assault guns were available for immediate deployment.

In early December the battalion was attached to 246.Volksgrenadier-Division, which had been fighting around Aachen, and by this time the first Jagdpanzer IV/70 (V) tank destroyers had arrived to supplement the assault guns, of which nineteen remained.

Schwere Panzerjäger-Abteilung 559. Formed on Monday, 10 April 1944 at Truppenübungsplatz Mielau, the battalion saw its first combat on 8 September when three Jagdpanthers were ambushed by Cromwell tanks of the Welsh Guards and at least one vehicle was quickly disabled.

The battalion was continuously engaged in the fighting in the Netherlands from early September until 8 December 1944, when it was withdrawn to Pronsfeld in Germany in preparation for the Ardennes Offensive. From 11 December 1944, the battalion was attached to Panzer-Lehr-Division and by that time the first company was equipped with fourteen Jagdpanthers while 3.Kompanie had been issued the battalion's first fifteen Jagdpanzer IV/70 tank destroyers earlier that month. Hauptmann Honold's 2.Kompanie controlled the remaining fourteen Sturmgeschütz III assault guns.

The German Army created several specialist armoured units during the war which were trained to clear minefields and eliminate enemy pillboxes and bunkers.

The first operations involved mine-detonating rollers but by May 1942 these had been superseded by a completely new radio-controlled vehicle capable of carrying a 500kg demolition charge under fire and placing it within a minefield or close to a target. Developed by the firm of Borgward, this was the schwerer Ladungsträger B IV Sd.Kfz 301 which, with slight variation, would remain in service until the end of the war. These vehicles were used with some success during Operation Citadel in June 1943 where, for the first time, they were controlled from specially adapted Sturmgeschütz III assault guns.

Panzer-Abteilung (Funklenk) 301. Formed in late 1942, the battalion served in Russia and Italy before being transferred to Truppenübungsplatz Grafenwöhr in Germany in mid-1944 to begin training on Tiger I tanks specially adapted to control the Borgward demolition vehicles.

In June, before the training was completed or the full allocation of vehicles was received, the battalion's 4.Kompanie was detached and sent to the Normandy front. The company was subordinated to 2.Panzer-Division and equipped with two Pzkpfw III command tanks, eight Sturmgeschütz III assault guns and thirty-six BIV remote control vehicles

Photographed in the town of Hertogenbosch, approximately thirty kilometres north of Eindhoven, this Sturmgeschütz III ausf G is almost certainly one of the assault guns of 3.Kompanie, schwere Panzerjäger-Abteilung 559 that attempted to secure the town in late October 1944. The heavy foliage camouflage was commonly seen on most German vehicles operating in Holland at this time.

Photographed in Holland in May 1945 this Sturmgeschütz III ausf G is one of the three surviving assault guns of 2.Kompanie, Panzerjäger-Abteilung 346. The brackets on the mudguard indicate that this vehicle was fitted with Schürzen at some time and other production features include the welded gun mantlet, the Rundumfeuer remotely-controlled machine gun, gun travel lock and rear stowage rack. The names on the hull front, Mitzi and Erika, probably represent girlfriends or female relatives and similar markings are also evident on the other vehicles. Note the sixteen kill markings on the barrel.

when the fighting commenced. In August 1944, the company returned to the Battalion which was reorganised as schwere Panzer-Abteilung (Tiger Funklenk) 301 and the assault guns were replaced by Tiger I tanks.

Panzer-Abteilung (Funklenk) 302. Formed in July 1944 with just four Sturmgeschütz III assault guns and three Befehlspanzer IV command tanks, the battalion served briefly in France and was transferred to the newly formed Panzerkorps Grossdeutschland later in the year.

Although 4.Kompanie, Panzer-Abteilung (Funklenk) 301, mentioned above, was ordered to join the battalion in late June as its first company, the order was very quickly altered and it is likely that the transfer never took place.

Panzer-Kompanie (Funklenk) 315. At the time of the Normandy landings this company was subordinated to 21.Panzer-Division and reported that ten Sturmgeschütz III and thirty-six Borgward demolition vehicles were ready for deployment. The company was involved in several major actions including the battles for the Carpiquet airfield and the fighting around Sainte-Honorine-la-Chardonne as part of Kampfgruppe von Luck. In late June thc company was withdrawn from the front and reorganised as 2.Kompanie, Panzer-Abteilung (Funklenk) 302.

Panzer-Kompanie (Funklenk) 316. Formed in July 1943, by the time of the Normandy invasion the battalion was attached to the Panzer-Lehr-Division. The company received the first five production models of the Tiger II tank in February 1944 and it was intended that these would replace the Sturmgeschütz III. The Tigers were found to be so mechanically unreliable that they were left at Chateuadun, south of Chartres, and the company fought the campaign with ten Sturmgeschütz III assault guns, three Tiger I tanks and fifty-four BIV remote control vehicles.

On 1 July 1944, the company was withdrawn and used to form Panzer Abteilung 302 (Funklenk).

Panzer-Kompanie (Funklenk) 319. This unit was the last of the independent Funklenk companies to be formed and was sent to the Western Front in September 1944, reporting that ten Sturmgeschütz III and thirty-six Borgward demolition vehicles were on hand. The company supported schwere Panzer-Abteilung (Tiger Funklenk) 301 in the defence of Merzenhausen, north-east of Aachen, and later fought in the Ardennes. In January it was used to form the third company of Panzer-Abteilung (Funklenk) 303.

A number of other Panzer units that were equipped at some time with the Sturmgeschütz should be at least mentioned here.

Führer-Grenadier-Brigade. Raised in July 1944 from elements of the Wolfschanze security detachment and replacements for the Grossdeutschland division, the brigade fought on the Eastern Front until September when it was transferred to the West. The 5.(Panzer) Kompanie was reorganised as a battalion,

.... continued on page 49

1. Sturmgeschütz III ausf G. 1.Batterie, Sturmgeschütz-Brigade 394. France, summer 1944. The guns of this battalion's first battery could be identified by a single number painted onto the superstructure side in a light colour, probably white, and usually outlined in black (2). Note the concrete applied around the commander's cupola and the rack used to hold lengths of spare track on the superstructure side.

1

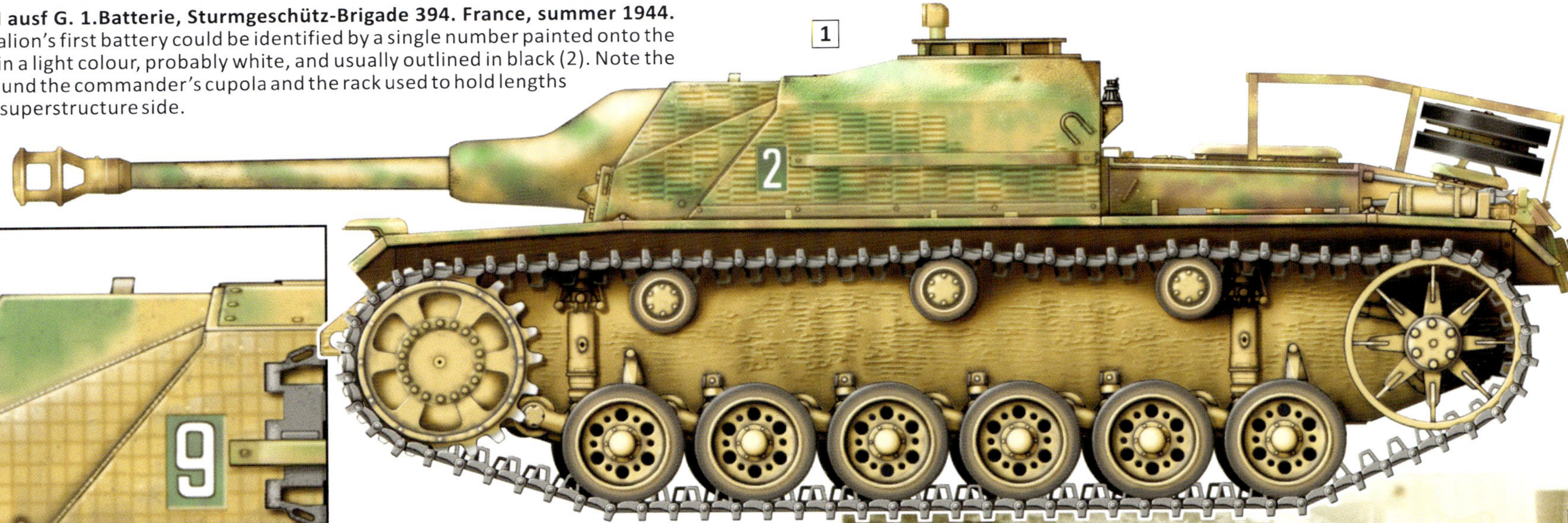

2

4

3. Sturmgeschütz III ausf G. 2.Batterie, Sturmgeschütz-Brigade 341. France, summer 1944. Disabled in the village of Le Val-Saint-Père on 31 July 1944, this vehicle was part of Kampfgruppe Bacherer, which was attempting to defend the bridge over the Sélune at Pontaubault.

3

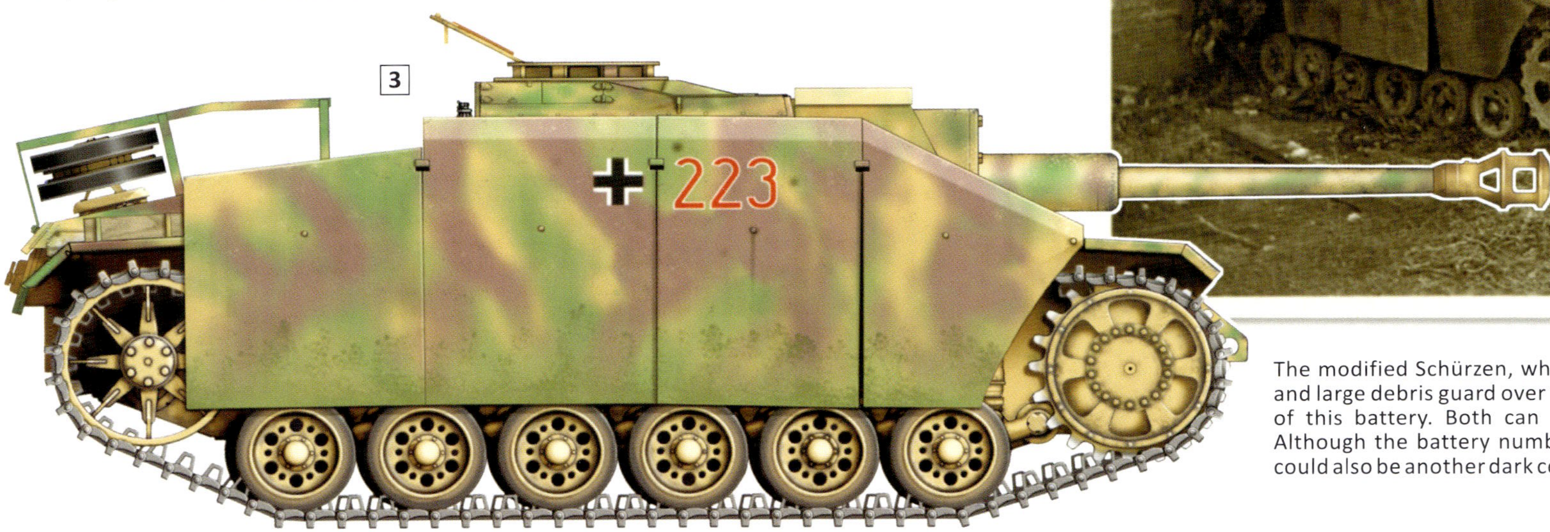

The modified Schürzen, which are bent inwards along the top edge, and large debris guard over the gun mantlet were identifying features of this battery. Both can be clearly seen in our photograph (4). Although the battery number is rendered here with a red centre it could also be another dark colour.

1

2

3
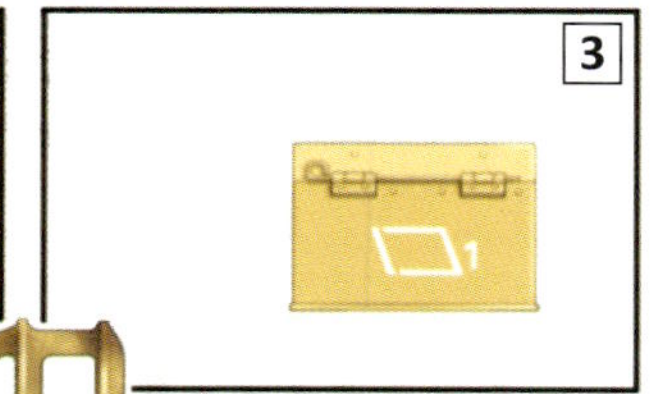

1. Sturmgeschütz IV. SS-Panzer-Abteilung 17. France, summer 1944. The battalion had forty-two of these assault guns on hand at the start of the Normandy campaign and it would seem that the appearance of most was similar to this vehicle with the only markings being the Balkenkeuz, a tactical symbol denoting a Panzer unit (2), combined with the company number and carried on the left front fender (3).

6

4. Sturmgeschütz III ausf G. 4.Kompanie, Panzer-Abteilung 301 (Funklenk). France, summer 1944. The deep wading exhaust system at the hull rear identifies this vehicle as one of 142 Pzkpfw III ausf M tanks that were converted to assault guns between February and November 1943. Only the battalion's 4.Kompanie was at the front during the Normandy battles and they could be identified by the tactical symbol and company number (5) painted onto the left front fender. This marking is also clearly visible in our photograph (6). Note the Zeltbahn tent quarter draped over the mantlet and what appears to be a metal cover behind the smoke candle dischargers.

4

5

1. Sturmgeschütz III ausf G. Sturmgeschütz-Abteilung 1243. France, summer 1944. This unit was in fact the second company of Panzerjager-Abteilung 243 and served in Normandy where all ten assault guns were lost. The style of numbering was consistent throughout the company and most, if not all, vehicles carried the Balkenkreuz national insignia on the superstructure side, although the exact position could vary. Gun barrels were coated in a black flame resistant laquer at the factory and it was not uncommon for these to be left unpainted by units in the field.

1

3

2. Sturmgeschütz III ausf G. SS-Panzer-Regiment 10. Holland, autumn 1944. Photographed in the streets of Brummen, north-east of Arnhem, this battered assault gun is one of the few serviceable vehicles that the regiment could field after the Normandy battles. Note the metal rack welded to the superstructure side and that the camouflage is extended to the area behind the suspension. A company number, which may be 202, is just visible on the hull rear in our photograph (3) as are, unusually, two Balkenkreuz national markings. The unit insignia is known to have been carried in the position shown here (4).

2

4

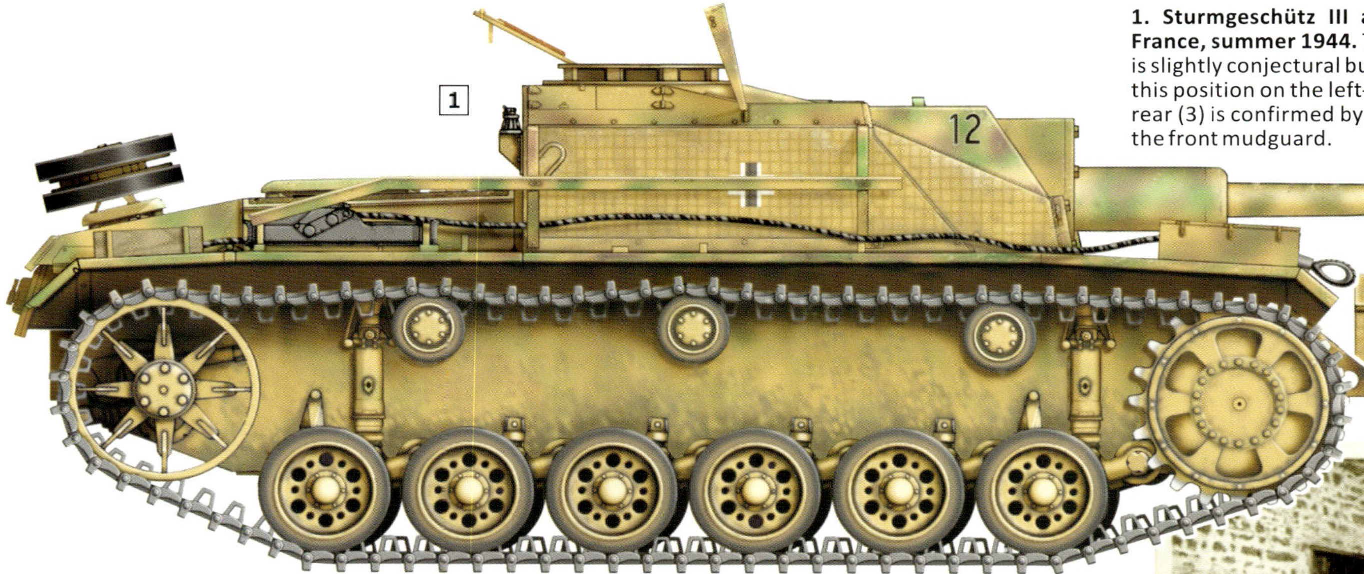

1

2

3

1. Sturmgeschütz III ausf G. Sturmgeschütz-Abteilung 1348. France, summer 1944. The number 12 on the superstructure side is slightly conjectural but these numbers were definitely carried in this position on the left-hand side. The unit insignia (2) on the hull rear (3) is confirmed by photographs. Note the toolbox welded to the front mudguard.

5

4

4. Sturmgeschütz III ausf G. SS-Sturmgeschütz-Abteilung 2. France, summer 1944. This assault gun was disabled and abandoned in the streets of Chambois, east of Falaise, during the final battles in Normandy and photographed from several angles. This Sturmgeschütz III has been fitted with additional concrete armour on either side of the main gun and the so-called swinging style Schürzen, both of which were thought to have been introduced much later in the year. Our photograph (5) shows the same vehicle after the hull Schürzen had been removed.

2

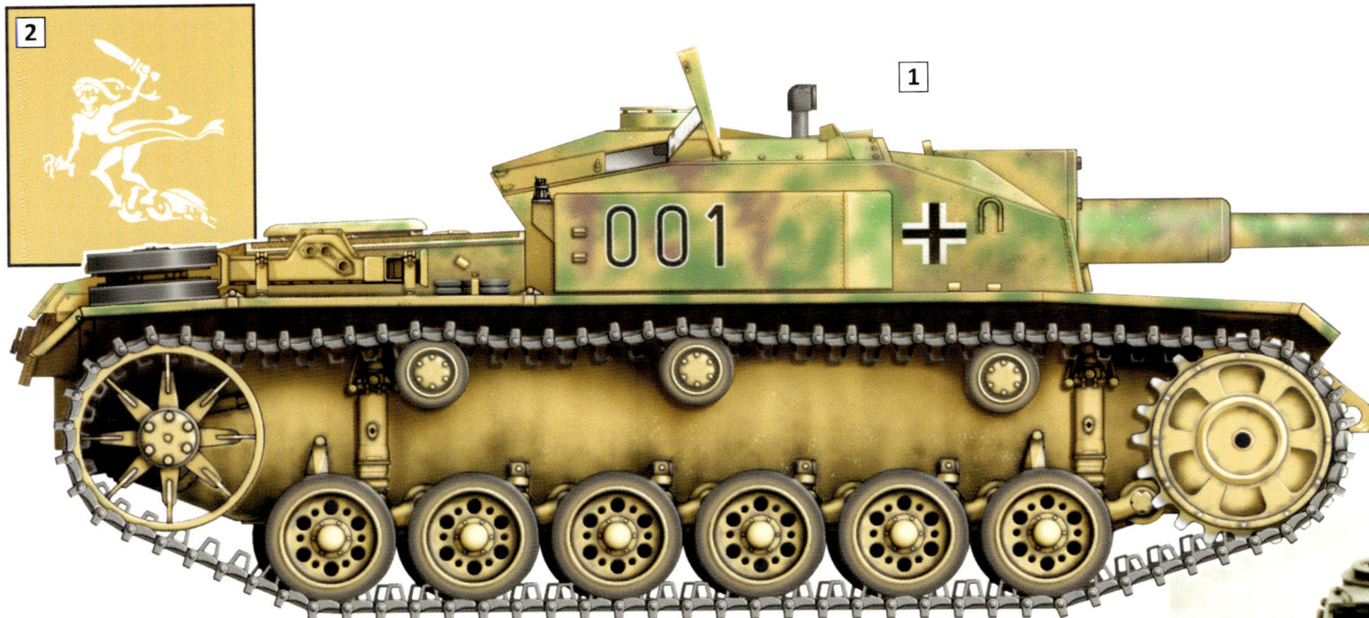

1

3

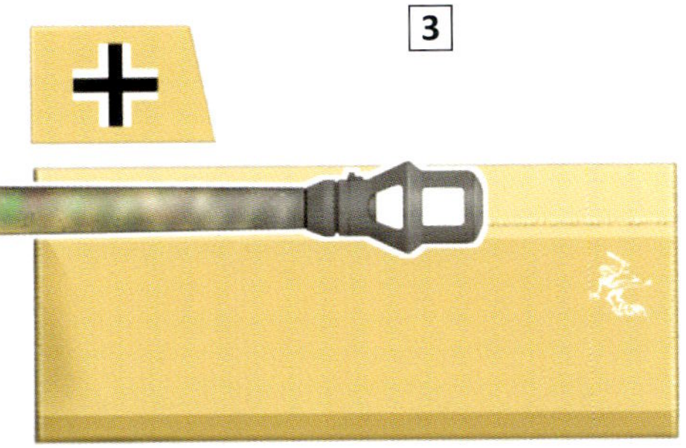

5

1. Sturmgeschütz III ausf F/8. Panzerjäger-Abteilung 61. France, autumn 1944. Disabled at Baume-les-Dames, on the road betwen Besançon and Belfort, this vehicle is one of eight operated by the Panzerjäger battalion of 11.Panzer-Division. These early model assault guns were not a common sight in the West by this time and this vehicle's markings are also slightly anachronistic with its large company number, slender Balkenkreuz and unit insignia (2), both of which were carried on the hull front (3).

4

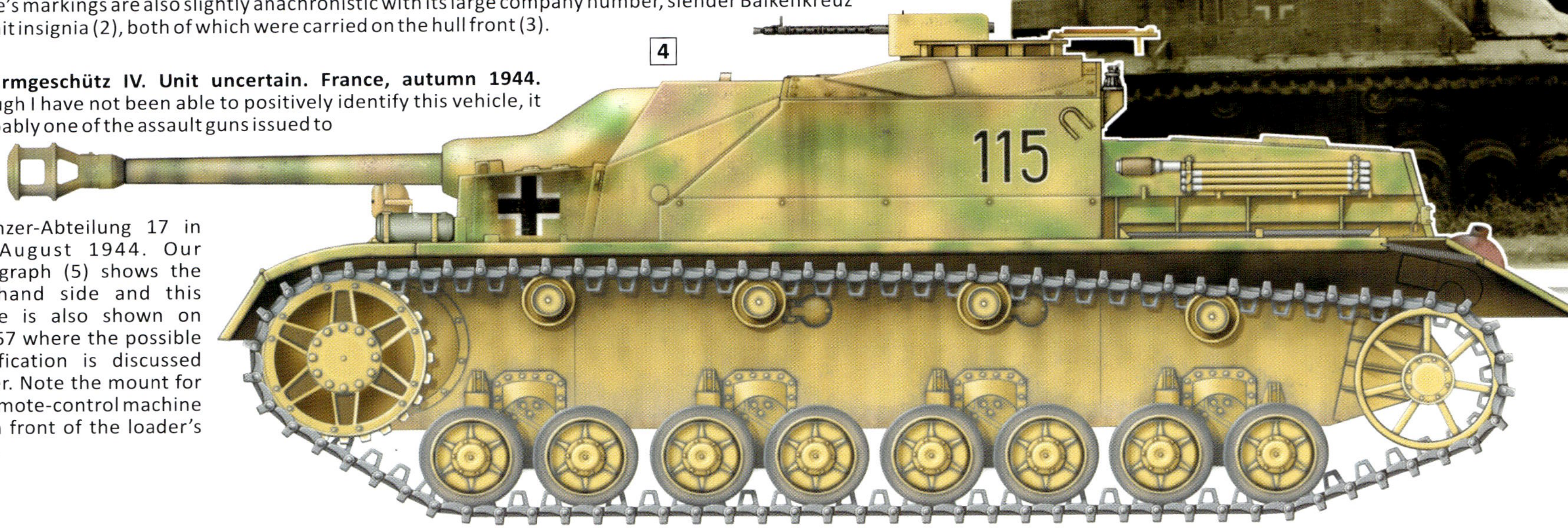

4. Sturmgeschütz IV. Unit uncertain. France, autumn 1944. Although I have not been able to positively identify this vehicle, it is probably one of the assault guns issued to SS-Panzer-Abteilung 17 in late August 1944. Our photograph (5) shows the right-hand side and this vehicle is also shown on page 57 where the possible identification is discussed further. Note the mount for the remote-control machine gun in front of the loader's hatch.

1

1. Sturmgeschütz III ausf G. 3.Batterie, Sturmgeschütz-Brigade 280. Holland, autumn 1944. The battalion's third battery, led by the Abteilungsführer Major Kurt Kühme, took part in the defence of Arnhem in September 1944. Photographic evidence would suggest that most of the vehicles did not carry any markings except, in rare instances, the Balkenkreuz national marking.

3

3. A photograph of the assault gun depicted at right. Note that the vehicle in the background has been painted in an identical pattern. Note that the suspension appears to have been painted in one of the darker camouflage colours.

2. Sturmgeschütz III ausf G. Unidentified unit. Holland, autumn 1944. Although I have not been able to identify the unit to which this vehicle belongs with any certainty, it may be 3.Kompanie, schwere Panzerjager-Abteilung 559 or Sturmgeschütz-Brigade 280. The intricate camouflage scheme is most unusual and it is possible to determine a pattern in the leaf motif suggesting that a stencil was used.

2

1. Sturmgeschütz III ausf G. III.Abteilung, Führer-Grenadier-Brigade. Luxembourg, winter 1944-45. This vehicle is also shown in the photograph on page 51 where it is possible to see the hole for the coaxial machine gun in the front plate of the welded gun mantlet introduced from June 1944. The lack of Zimmerit paste would suggest that this assault gun was assembled after mid-September 1944. The three-colour camouflage, dominated by the darker shades, is common for this period. The brigade's unit insignia (2) shown here was probably not carried by the battalion's assault guns but is included as a matter of interest.

1

2

3. Sturmgeschütz III ausf G. 1.Kompanie, Panzer-Abteilung 103. Belgium, winter 1944-45. Attached to 3.Panzergrenadier-Division the battalion had recently been transferred from Italy and was at almost full strength at the beginning of the Ardennes Offensive. The method of displaying the company number was common throughout the battalion (4) and the division's unit insignia (5) may have been carried by some assault guns on the hull front as it certainly was in Italy. The large box on the hull rear also seems to have been a common feature.

4

3

5

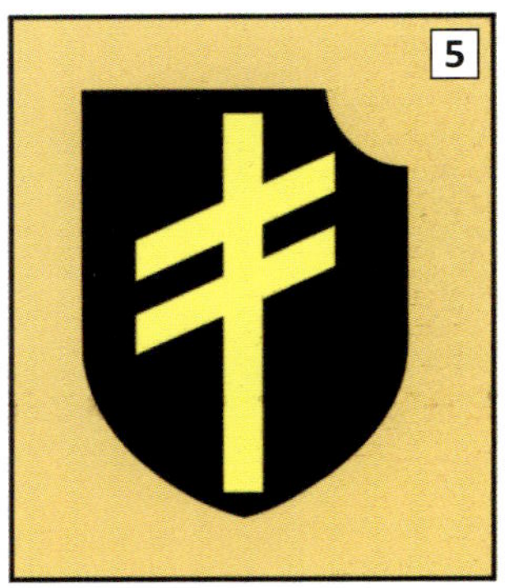

1. Sturmgeschütz III ausf G. Fallschirm-Sturmgeschütz-Brigade 11. Luxembourg, winter 1944-45. Disabled during the fighting around the village of Flatzbourhof, north of Holtz, this assault gun is painted in what may be one of the factory-applied camouflage schemes introduced in late 1944. However, it is obvious from the available photographic evidence that some units in the field created their own versions of the so-called Ambush scheme and the homemade appearance of many, as can be seen from our photograph (2), is obvious. The white dots are almost certainly a latter addition.

1

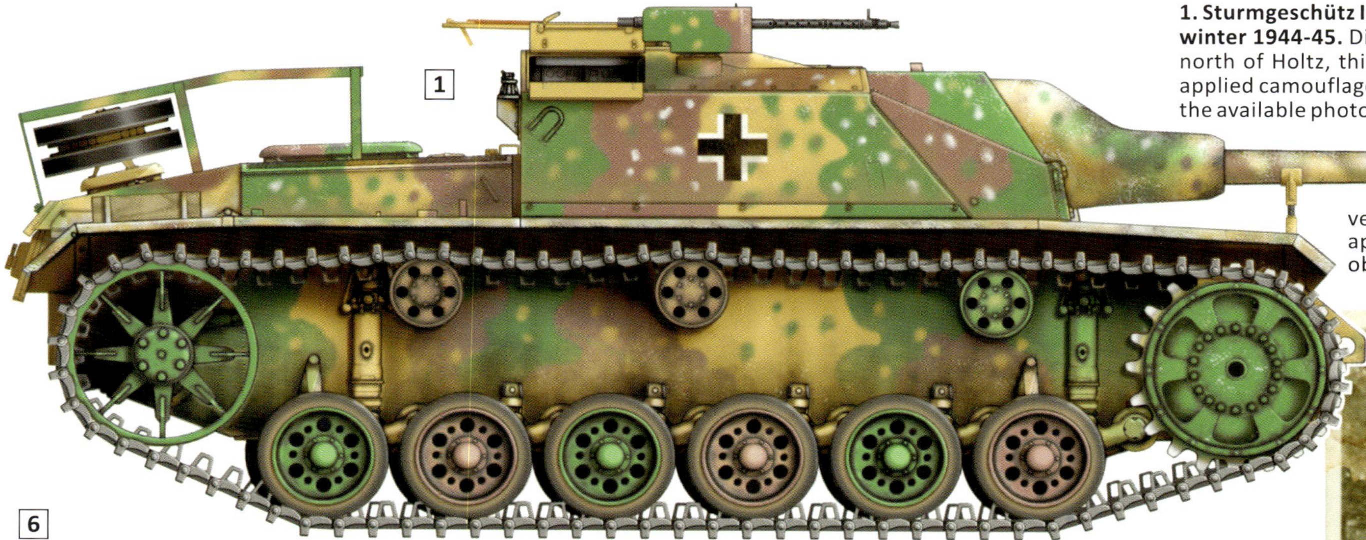

2

3. Sturmgeschütz III ausf G. Heeres-Sturmartillerie-Brigade 667. Belgium, winter 1944-45. The Fahrgestellnummer, 197012, painted in black on the hull front (4) would seem to suggest that this vehicle's camouflage was applied at the factory. Note that the additional concrete armour has not been painted, lending further credence to the claim that this assault gun was camouflaged before it left the assembly plant. The battalion's colourful unit insignia (5) was carried at both the front and rear (6). This Sturmgeschütz III is also shown in the photograph on page 10.

6

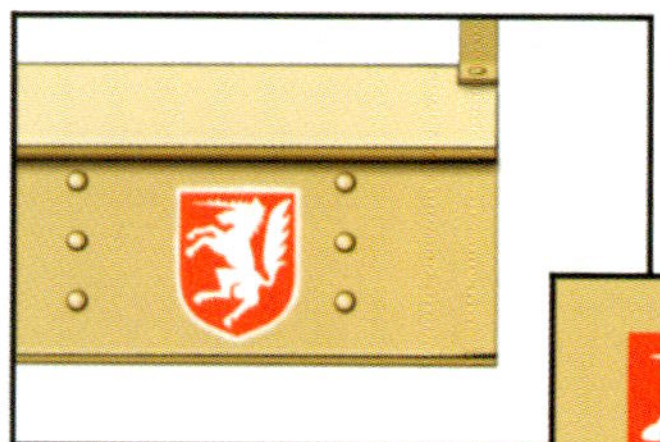

5

3

4

1. Sturmgeschütz III ausf G. Unidentified unit. France, winter 1944-45. Photographed near Thionville, which was part of the Metz defensive system, this assault gun may have belonged to the Panzerjäger battalions of either 19.Volksgrenadier-Division or 25.Panzergrenadier-Division. In the photograph on which this illustration is based the bracket for the hull Schürzen has been almost completely blown away (2) but I have included It here as it would have appeared.

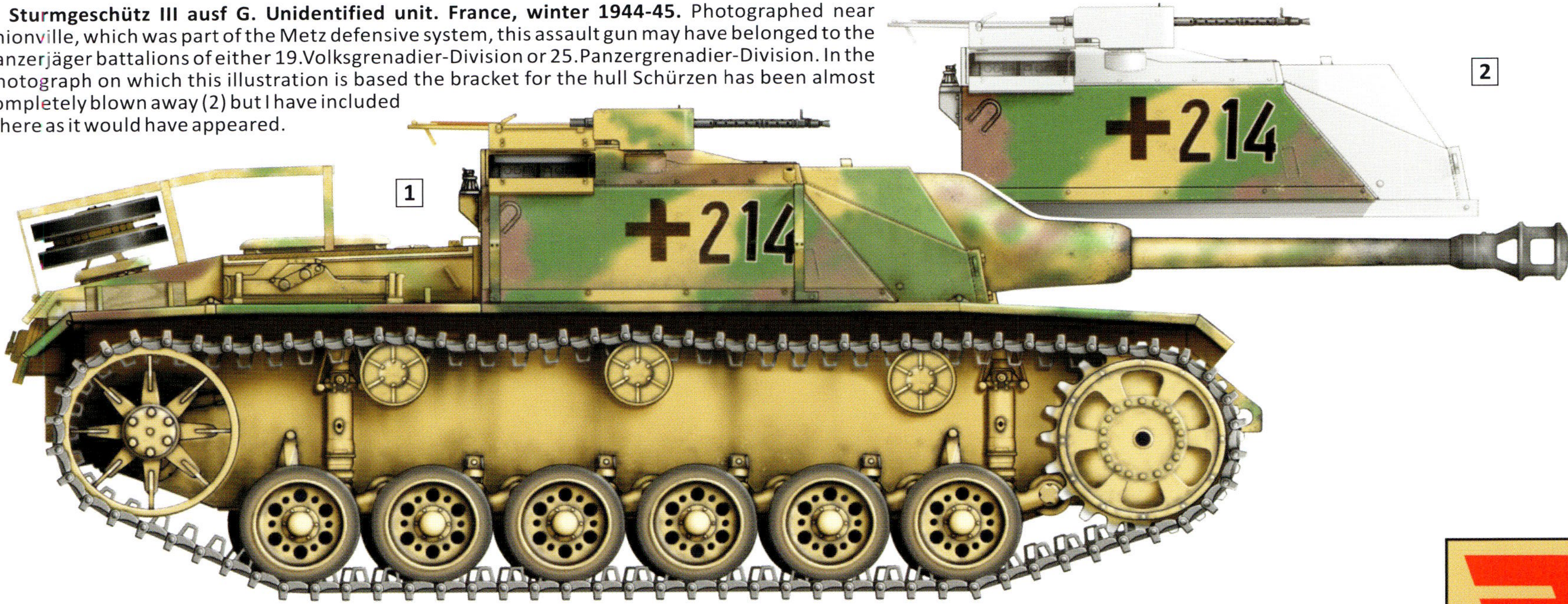

3. Sturmgeschütz IV. Sturmgeschütz-Abteilung 1353. Germany, spring 1945. The battalion reported that nineteen Sturmgeschütz IV assault guns were on hand in January 1945 and it is probable that 1.(Panzerjäger) Kompanie and 2.(Sturmgeschütz) Kompanie, referred to a s

Sturmgeschütz-Abteilung 1353, were both equipped with these vehicles. This unusual organisation would explain the company number of 112. The unit insignia of the battalion's parent formation, 353.Infanterie-Division (4), is shown here as a matter of interest only.

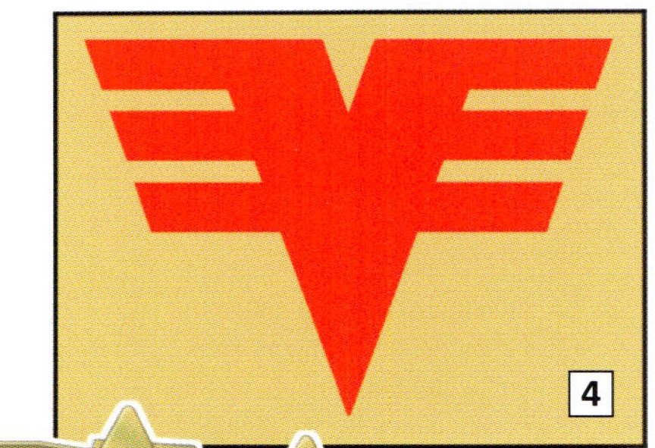

1. Sturmgeschütz III ausf G. Panzer-Lehr-Abteilung Bergen. Germany, spring 1945. This ad-hoc unit was raised from elements of Panzertruppen-Schule II at Bergen-Fallingbostel and fought in the last weeks of the war around Kassel. The mount for the Rundumsfeuer machine gun confirms that this vehicle was assembled after March 1944 but it has no Zimmerit coating or even camouflage paint. Note the method of holding the spare track links to the superstructure side.

1

3

2. Sturmgeschütz III ausf G. Unidentified unit. Germany, spring 1945. The style of Schürzen shown here had become increasingly common by 1945. This system, where the metal plates pivoted on a pipe welded to the mudguards (3), may have begun as a field modification but there is no doubt that it had been adopted by the factories by the last months of the war. The style of camouflage depicted here was also frequently encountered on both fronts at this time and may have been applied at the assembly plants. Note the aperture for the coaxial machine gun in the Topfblende mantlet identifying this assault gun as a post-October 1944 vehicle.

2

1

1. Sturmgeschütz III ausf F/8. Unidentified unit. Germany, spring 1945. When older model armoured vehicles were returned to Germany for major repairs they were usually upgraded with the most recent modifications and this Sturmgeschütz has been fitted with a full set of the early style Schürzen and brackets. Many of these early production vehicles were allocated to training establishments and eventually used to create ad-hoc Kampfgruppen in the last days of the war.

3

4

2. Sturmgeschütz III ausf G. 2.Kompanie, Panzer-Abteilung 103. Germany, spring 1945. Photographed outside the village of Modrath, west of Cologne, the distinctive method of displaying this vehicle's company number on the front (3) and rear (4) hull identifies the unit as the Panzer battalion of 3.Panzergrenadier-Division. The camouflage pattern, made up of diagonal lines of Olivgrün, Rotbraun and Dunkelgelb, applied with a soft edge, was typical of the late war factory-applied schemes.

2

STUG IV

LATE PRODUCTION

1/35 SCALE

ROLAND SORGNER

Austrian modeller Roland Sorgner's build depicts a late production Sturmgeschütz IV fitted with the brackets to the so-called Thoma Schürzen. These were made up of wire mesh panels and an example is shown in the photograph at the top of the page attached to a Pzkpfw IV ausf J.

Roland's model was made with parts from Dragon Models' Pzkpfw IV kit released in 1995, Italeri's StuG IV and the 1987 Academy StuG IV kit which was a re-boxing of a Tamiya model. The drive sprockets, road wheels and tracks are all from Dragon while the remainder of the suspension was taken from various kits.

The brackets for the Thoma Schürzen were scratchbuilt from aluminium tube and plastic strips and a number of pieces from the ubiquitous spare parts box.

Below: 1. The main gun mantlet and gun travel lock. 2. The Bosch headlight and fire extinguisher. 3. Another shot of the gun mantlet showing the aperture for the coaxial machine gun. 4. The ventilator on the rear of the superstructure and the remotely-controlled machine gun.

1

2

3

4

The assembled model was spray-painted with Tamiya Acrylics XF-64 Red Brown and XF-5 Flat Green fade with either XF-60 Flat White or XF-67 Buff and a generous amount of thinner. Once painted, the model was weathered with Roland's unique mixture of dried tea leaves, ground to a fine powder, and blended with rice powder, sugar or chalk. To vary the colours Roland then adds coloured artist's chalk.

The extremely convincing mud and dirt was achieved by mixing the ground tea leaves with Revell Enamel 87.

STUG III
AUSF G
LATE PRODUCTION
1/35 SCALE
QI BIN

1

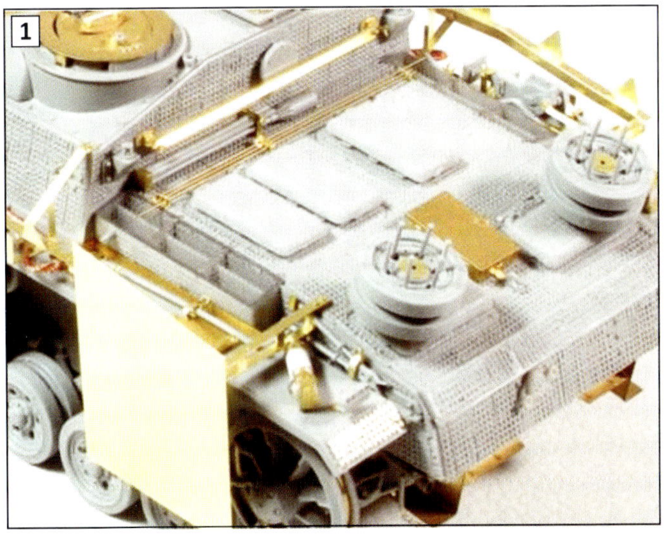

2

Chinese modeller Qi Bin's late production Sturmgeschütz III was built for E.T. Model, which is featured on page 46, and was based on the Dragon Models' 1/35 scale kit and two of E.T. Model's photo-etched upgrade sets. Shown here are, 1 and 2. Parts from E.T. Model's E35-226 photo-etched brass set, a basic StuG III upgrade. 3. The first stage of the camouflage with the markings applied. 4. Details of the E35-226 set which is a more comprehensive upgrade featuring extra parts. 5. The partly-assembled model painted in a Dunkelgelb base coat.

3

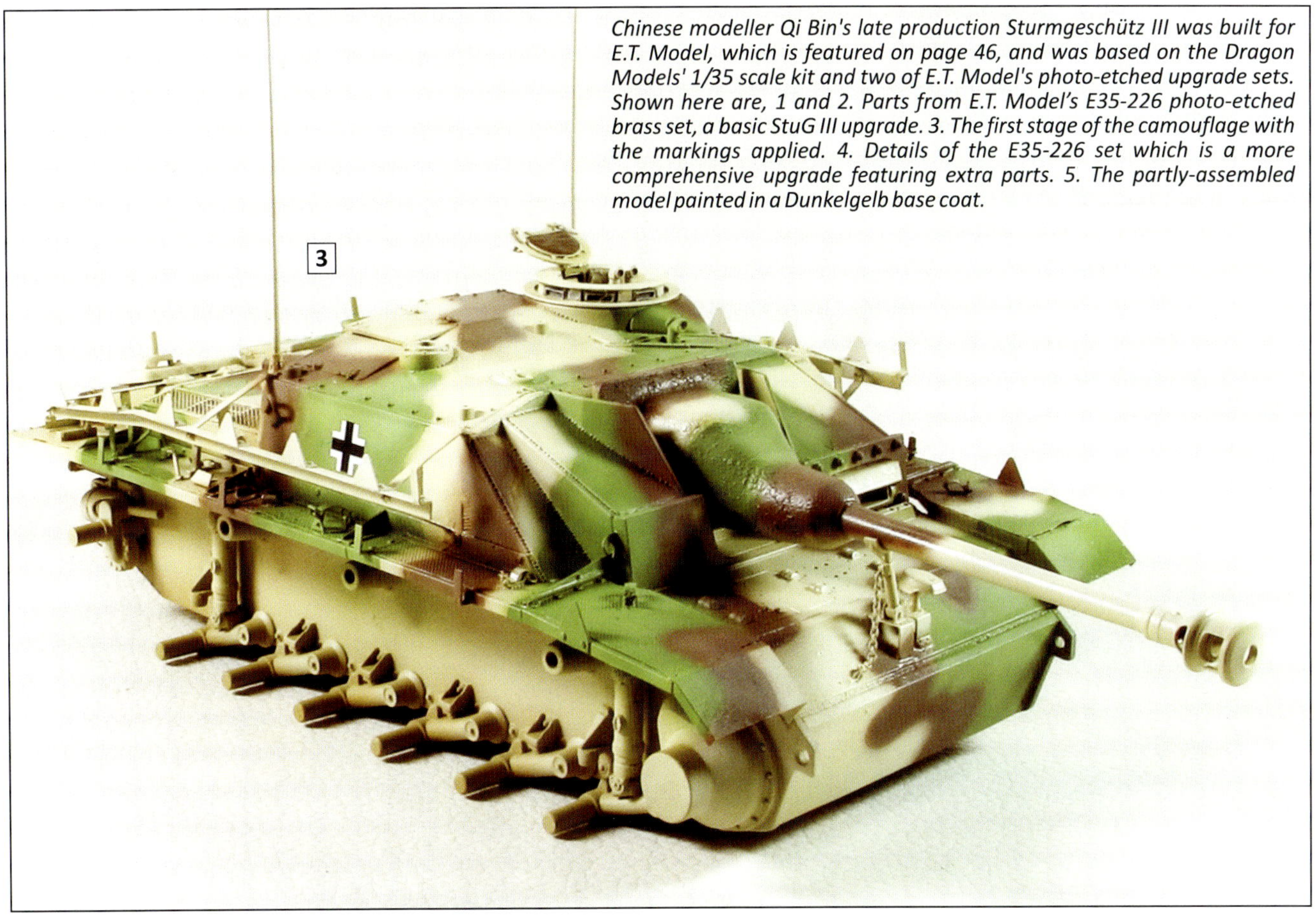

4

5

The completed model showing the later style brackets for the hull Schürzen but without the individual armour plates which remain detachable. This replica is replete with small details including the tow cables, retaining chain for the gun travel lock, commander's periscope and track pins holding the spare wheels on the hull rear.

At right: The completed model with the hull Schürzen in place. Below: Details of the partly completed model after it had been coated in its Dunkelgelb base coat. Mr Hobby paints were used to create the camouflage pattern and AMMO by Mig Jimenez products were used for the weathering and mud.

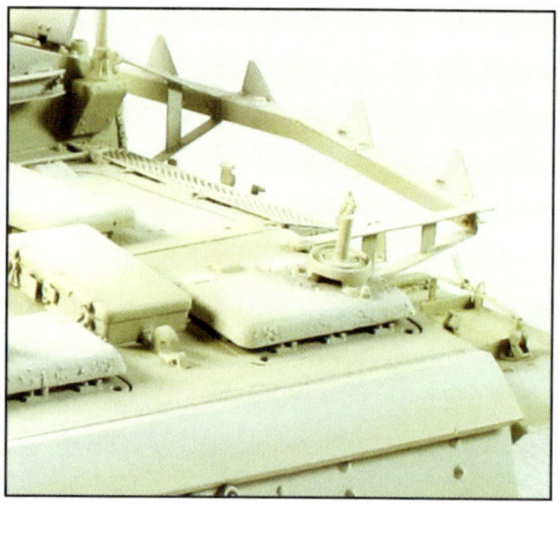

STUG III

ALKETT AUSF G

WESTERN FRONT 1944

1/35 SCALE

NAOMASA DAIRAKU

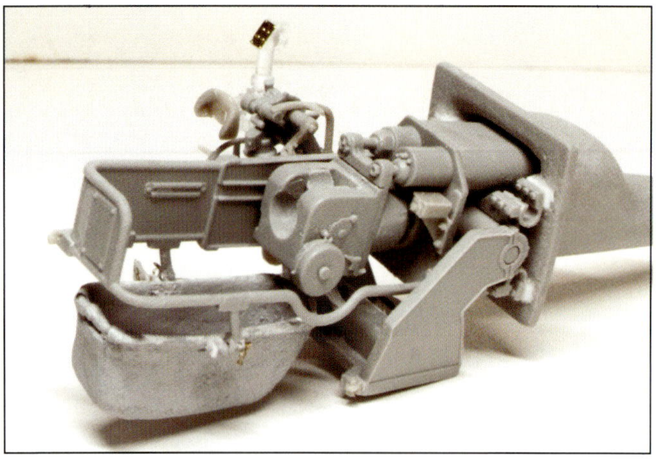

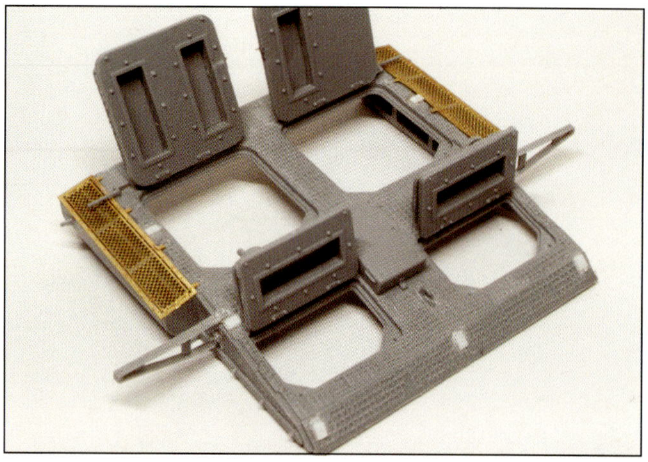

Japanese modeller Naomasa Dairaku's build is based on the Dragon Model's 1/35 scale kit completed with photo-etched parts from Aber with interior details from CMK Kits, a Czech company which has been featured in other books in this series. Many small parts were scratchbuilt from plastic tubing and card.

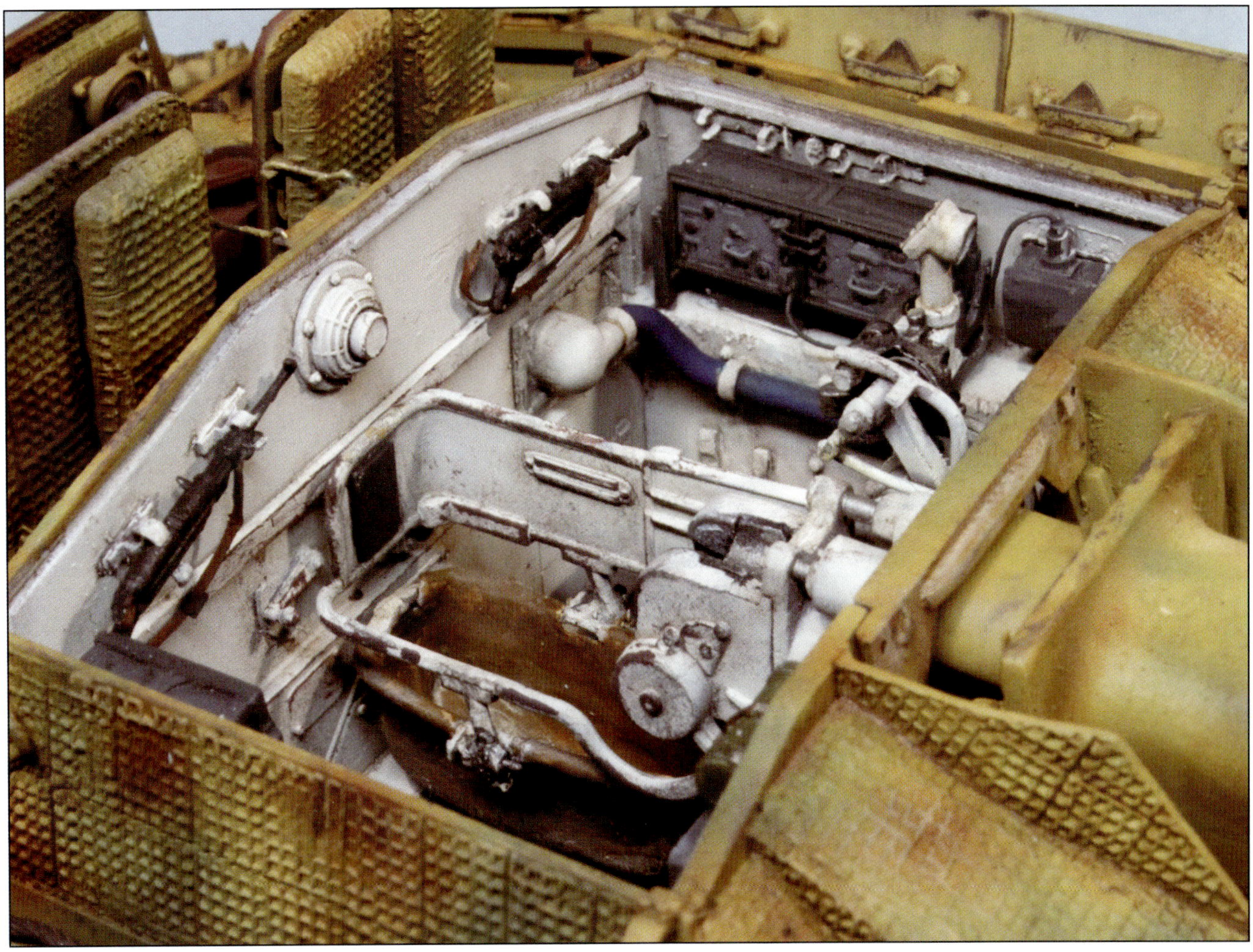

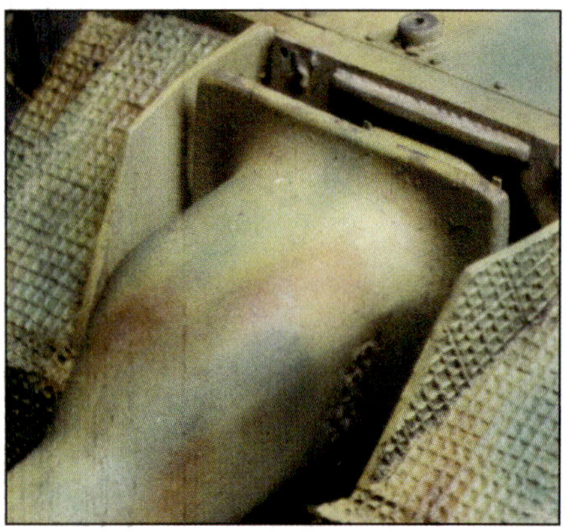

The model's base colour and camouflage were created with Gaia Color, a range of paints and lacquers popular with Japanese modellers, using an airbrush. Naomasa then painted the intricate camouflage with a fine brush by hand. The tracks are from Modelkasten. This vehicle is also shown and discussed in the Camouflage & Markings section on page 22.

Although perhaps not as glamorous as the Tiger and Panther tanks, the Sturmgeschütz assault gun has been a constant favourite with modellers since plastic armour kits became readily available in the 1960s. Indeed, one of the best-known kits from this early period, Airfix's StuG III Assault Gun in 1/76 scale, is still selling today. One of the first large scale models, Monogram's 1/32 scale StuG IV released in 1968, was this author's first serious attempt at armour modelling after being inspired by a 'how-to' article written by the great Shepard Paine.

The shortcomings of these early kits are all too obvious today but they should perhaps be judged only after considering the limitations of the period, both in the technology of mould making and in the paucity of reliable research material.

The 1970s was something of a Golden Age for plastic model collectors and builders, with firms such as Midori, Otaki, Eidai and Bandai in Japan and ESCI in Europe offering relatively accurate replicas at a reasonable price. It was also at this time that Tamiya, after some experimentation, decided that its armour models would henceforth all be produced in 1/35 scale, an aspect of the hobby that Tamiya controlled for some time. But it was in 1989 that Gunze Sangyo released the first of would be called multi-media kits which contained injection-moulded plastic parts, photo-etched details, individual track links and other additional options. One of the first subjects of this range was a 1/35 scale Sturmgeschütz III ausf G. At about this time ESCI was transforming its small scale range by introducing hard plastic tracks and Dragon Models, a newcomer from Hong Kong, was making an impact as modellers were demanding greater accuracy and detail.

Models of the StuG III and StuG IV are today produced in a number of scales from tiny 6mm wargames miniatures to the huge, radio-controlled 1/6 scale versions but these are at the extreme ends of the market and I have chosen to concentrate here, as in previous books, on the most popular modelling scales of 1/35, 1/48 and 1/72. The expansion of the market in recent years has also contributed to the proliferation of smaller, specialised companies producing accessories in resin, photo-etched metal, plastic, wood and other materials allowing a level of super-detailing which had previously been the province of a few master modellers. This list is of course far from exhaustive, mostly due to reasons of space and the almost constant flow of new releases and I would urge readers to undertake their own research using the index of manufacturers and their contact details can be found on page 64.

TAMIYA INCORPORATED

This Japanese company, which began life as a sawmill, has been manufacturing plastic kits since 1959, releasing their first armour model two years later. By the early 1970s Tamiya was producing a large range of armoured vehicles and accessories and the company was almost solely responsible for the rise in popularity of 1/35 scale. Like Airfix, the adoption of a constant scale proved popular at a time when many manufacturers were making models to fit the box in which they would eventually be marketed.

Tamiya's early kits were, for their day, highly detailed, relatively easy to assemble and, most importantly, affordable. From 2003 Tamiya began releasing a series of armour models in 1/48 scale, including early and late models of the Sturmgeschütz III, and this line has been extremely successful for the company.

At left, from top to bottom: The 1/48 scale early StuG III ausf G. The mid-production version StuG III in 1/35 scale. Tamiya's StuG IV, also in 1/35 scale. At right: A detail of the StuG IV hull and superstructure.

Below: Tamiya's StuG III ausf G in 1/48 scale built and painted according to the kit instructions as a vehicle of Sturmgeschütz-Brigade 237.

DRAGON MODELS LTD

Dragon Models was one of the first of the major manufacturers to offer accurate replicas in 1/35 scale and their kits are today something of a benchmark. The company's small scale releases are some of the best available. At the time of writing this Hong Kong based company offered twenty-nine construction kits of the StuG III and StuG IV, including a Sturmhaubitze 42, in 1/35 scale and nine kits in 1/72 scale. It should be mentioned that many of these kits utilise common parts and are sometimes re-boxings with different markings and additional parts. Dragon Models also offer a number of assembled and pre-painted models of the StuG III and StuG IV in 1/72 scale.

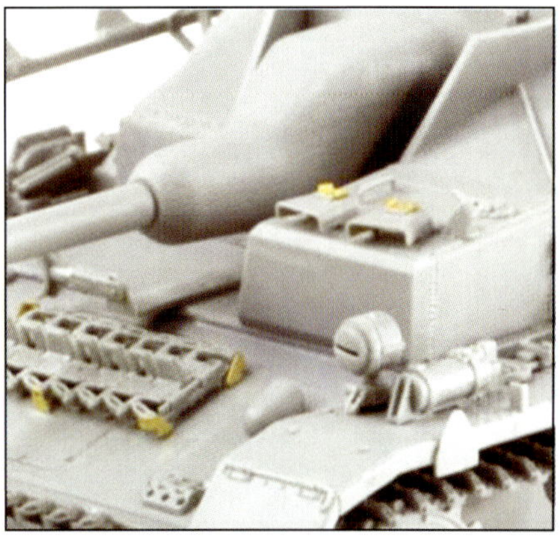

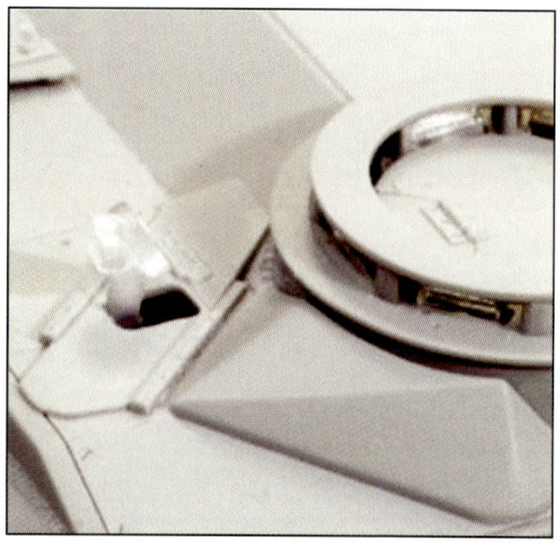

Above: Details of Dragon Models' 1/35 scale StuG IV including the driver's compartment and periscopes, flame-dampening exhaust mufflers and commander's cupola. Below: The 1/35 scale StuG III ausf G built with the Eduard Model Accessories photo-etched brass set.

Below: Details of Dragon Models' 1/35 scale StuG III ausf G including the interior and breech of the main gun.

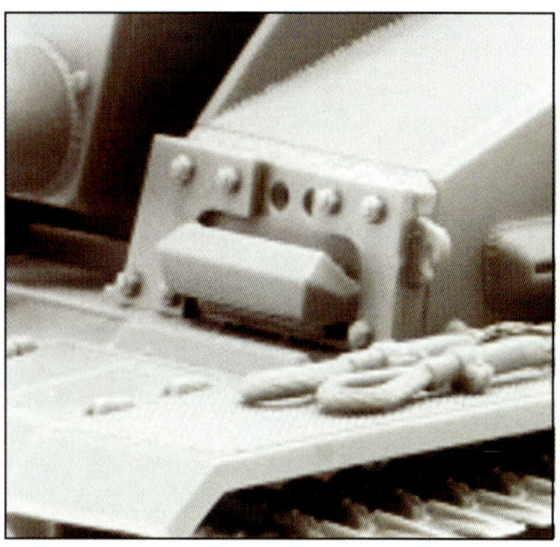

TRUMPETER/HOBBY BOSS

Often thought to be separate entities, these Chinese companies are in fact owned by the same corporation, are located at the same address and are essentially the same firm although different models are marketed separately under the two labels. Although the company now seems to be concentrating on modern subjects, Trumpeter does offer a number of 1/72 scale StuG III models. Shown below are, 1. The StuG IV. 2. The StuG III ausf F. 3. Part of the StuG III ausf F hull which is also used for the other early variants produced by Trumpeter.

1

2

3

ACADEMY

Based in Korea, this company produces an extensive range of military miniatures in both 1/35 and 1/72 scale. The current catalogue includes a 1/35 scale StuG IV which was originally released in 1987. In 2018, after extensive re-tooling, the kit was re-released with new box art and markings. Shown below are, 1. The box of the original 1987 kit. 2. The completed 2018 model in a rather fanciful colour scheme. 3. A detail of the current model. 4. The kit built from the box.

1

3

4

2

ITALERI

This Italian company has been producing plastic models since its foundation in 1962 and the current catalogue contains a 1/35 scale StuG IV which was originally released in 1980. Although this kit has been re-released over the years, and also marketed under the Zvezda and Revell labels, it has changed little. In 1/72 scale Italeri produces a StuG III ausf G which is the old ESCI kit that can also be built as a Sturmhaubitze 42. Of the larger model manufacturers Italeri alone has ventured into 1/56 scale with a reasonable accurate and detailed rendition of the StuG III ausf. This scale complements 28mm wargames figures of which there are now quite a number on the market. A number of Italeri's armour models have also been released under the World of Tanks label.

Above: Italeri's 1/35 scale Sturmgeschütz IV model in its most recent re-boxing. The photo-etched brass details visible here are all included with the kit as are the white metal tracks and an aluminium barrel for the 7.5cm gun.

BRONCO

Actually a subsidiary of the Ningbo Weijun Plastic Moulding Company, Bronco released its first kit in 2004. The current catalogue offers a number of early war variants and and a StuG III ausf C/D upgraded with the long 7.5cm L/48 gun and Topfblende mantlet. Shown below are the built StuG III ausf E model with the box art of the StuG III ausf C/D conversion.

REVELL

This company has been producing plastic models for almost as long as Airfix and was at one time known for its highly detailed and accurate replicas. The current catalogue contains a 1/35 scale StuG IV, which was mentioned under the Italeri heading, a StuG III ausf G and a StuG III ausf F/8, which are both re-boxings of Dragon Models kits. The company's 1/72 scale StuG III was first released in 2003 but it is stil a good and reasonably priced representation and was upgraded with some extra parts in 2013 and released as a late production vehicle.

Above, left to right: Revell's late production StuG III in 1/72 scale. A later re-isse of the late production kit with new markings. The 1/35 scale StuG IV which is a re-boxing of the Italeri model.

Above, left to right: Revell's 1/72 scale late production StuG III built with the upgrade set from Black Dog.

AIRFIX

No listing of model replicas of the Sturmgeschütz would be complete without at least some mention of the venerable Airfix 1/76 scale kit. First released in 1962, the packaging and box art has changed many times over the intervening years, as has the ownership of the company, although the model itself has remained completely unaltered, including the marking options. The soft plastic tracks, which generations of modellers have complained about endlessly, could only be described as rudimentary and are impervious to any glue. But it was, for its day, an accurate representation of an important armoured vehicle and the starting point for many armour modellers.

Below: Airfix's 1/76 scale StuG III, or 75mm Assault Gun, built recently for the company's catalogue. At left: One of the many re-packagings of this kit, shown here is the 1963 version. By 1965 the plastic bags had been replaced by cardboard boxes.

EDUARD MODEL ACCESSORIES

This Polish company has been manufacturing high-quality accessories in photo-etched brass and resin for many years and was one of the earliest firms to offer upgrade sets in the smaller scales. In addition to the upgrade sets Eduard offers other accessories including metal gun barrels, scale rifles and machine guns, ammunition crates, paint masks and markings.

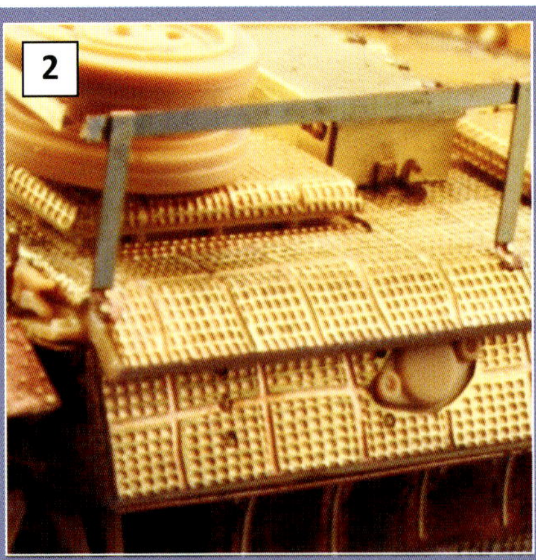

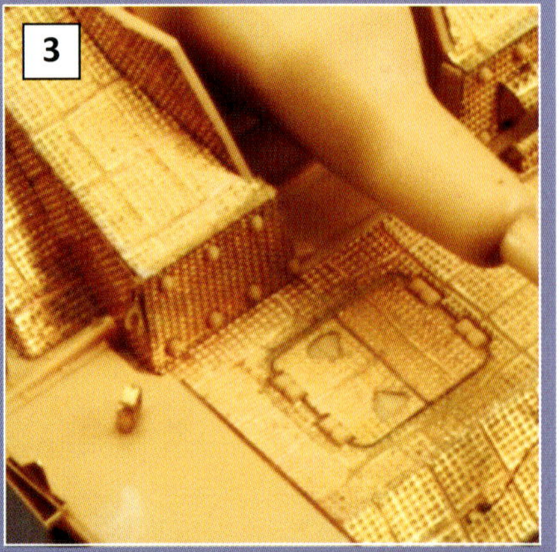

Above, 1. Details of the 1/35 scale upgrade set showing the shield for the remote-control machine gun, internal hatch parts and cupola periscopes. 2.and 3. The so-called Waffle pattern Zimmerit applied to Tamiya's 1/48 scale StuG III. Below: The comprehensive photo-etched brass detail set shown here with Dragon Models' 1/35 scale StuG IV.

Below, left: Parts of the interior hatch details. Below, right: Another shot of Dragon's 1/35 scale StuG IV built with the Eduard photo-etched brass detail set, this time including the hull Schürzen and brackets.

HAULER

Based in the Czech Republic, this company produces accessory sets in photo-etched brass and resin in 1/48, 1/35 and even 1/87 scale, a size which complements HO scale railway models. A number of items in the company's extensive range are now produced under the Bren Gun logo. Shown below are parts of the photo-etched brass and resin upgrade sets produced to complement the Tamiya 1/48 scale StuG III including hull Schurzen, loader's machine gun shield, engine grills and rear hull stowage rack. Also visible are the very finely detailed tool clasps and buckles.

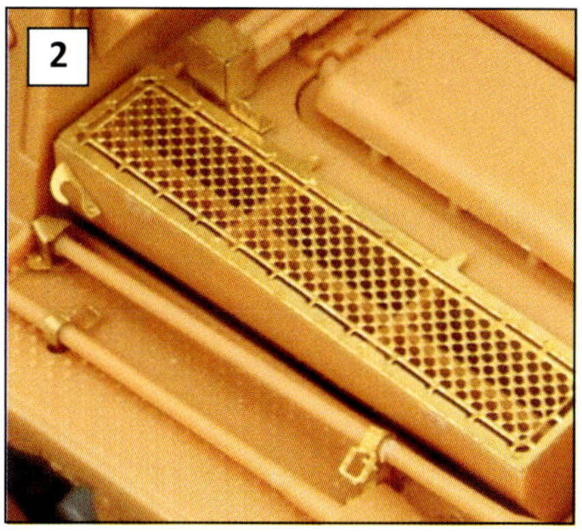

GRIFFON MODEL

Based in China this company produces a large range of photo-etched brass sets for the StuG III and StuG IV in 1/35 scale to fit most manufacturers' kits, although they do recommend the models of Tamiya and Dragon. Some sets are quite basic, for example containing a machine-gun shield and ammunition drum, while others are extremely comprehensive and are made up of hundreds of brass and resin parts. The photogrpahs below all depict details of the company's Premium Edition upgrade set for an Alkett-produced StuG III in 1/35 scale.

BLACK DOG

Based in the Czech Republic this company produces a large range of detailed resin accessory and upgrade sets for armoured vehicles in 1/35, 1/48 and 1/72 scale and a small number of complete kits. Shown below are, 1. and 2. The accessory set for Dragon Models' 1/72 scale StuG III ausf G. 3. and 4. Resin details for the Tamiya 1/48 scale StuG III ausf G. 5. The 1/48 scale Tamiya StuG III ausf B built with Black Dog details. 6. The resin set for a 1/35 scale StuG III ausf C/D.

E.T. MODEL

This relatively new manufacturer from China produces upgrade sets in 1/72 and 1/35 scale in brass and resin. Most sets are specifically designed, according to the company, to fit Dragon or Tamiya kits but most would be appropriate for other manufacturers' kits. The company also offers a large number of diorama pieces including fuel drums and canisters, various types of baggage, photo-etched barbed wire and even garden furniture and leaves in 1/35, 1/48 and 1/72 scale. Recent releases from Meng-Models have included photo-etched parts from E.T. Model

VOYAGER MODEL

Voyager have been manufacturing comprehensive upgrade sets for scale models since 2003 with the release of their first set for 1/35 scale armour. The company also produces turned aluminium barrels with muzzle brakes for both the late and early 7.5cm main guns of the StuG in 1/35 scale and accessories in resin including a detailed commander's cupola. Shown below are, 1. Late Schürzen and additional armour in 1/35 scale. 2. Parts of the detail set fro the Dragon Models 1/35 scale StuG III. 3. Photo-etched brass and resin details applied to the Dragon Models StuG IV.

RB MODEL

RB Model from Poland produce a range of milled aluminium and brass gun barrels and resin accessories for 1/72, 1/48 and 1/35 scale armour models. Shown below are, 1. The beautifully detailed 1/35 scale barrel and late-pattern muzzle brake for the 7.5cm L/48 gun which armed the StuG III and StuG IV. 2. The barrel for an MG 34, also in 1/35 scale. 3. A selection of shells for the 7.5cm gun, both armour-piercing and high explosive, in 1/72 scale. More generic items include highly detailed towing shackles, radio antenna insulators and fuel drums.

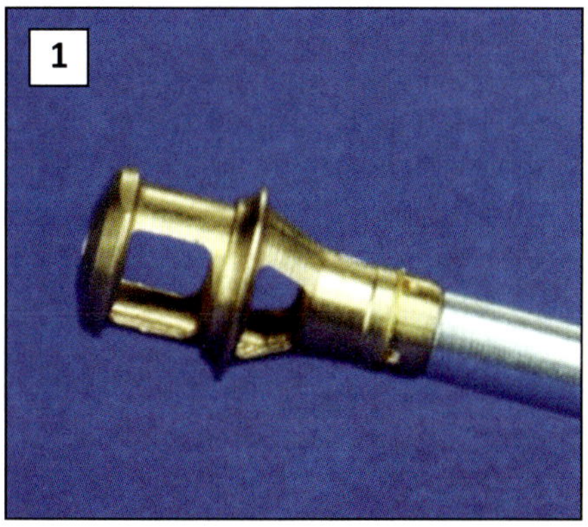

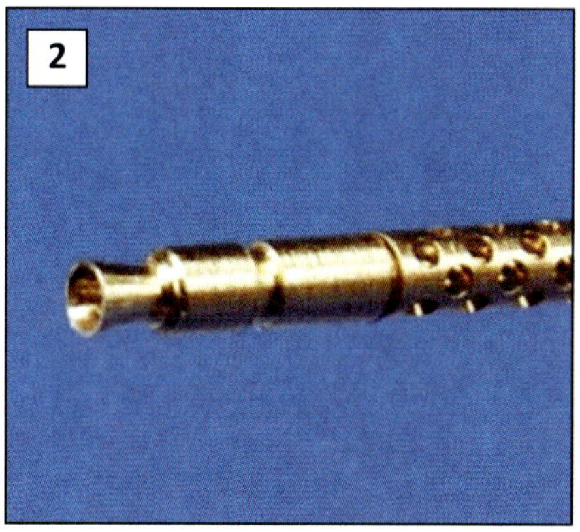

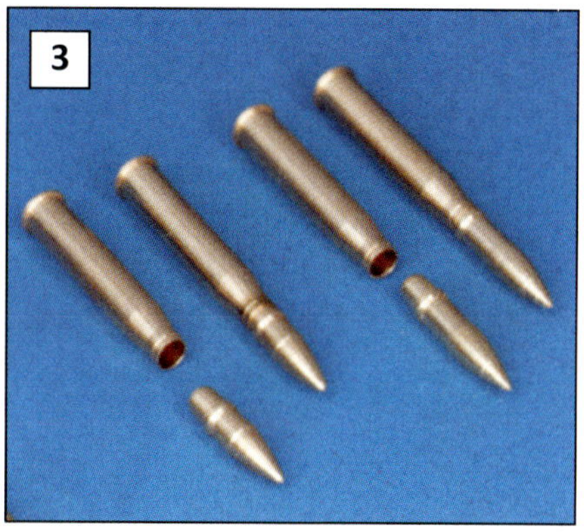

JK RESIN

This Czech company has been producing a large range of 1/72 scale kits and accessories for some time and many of its older offerings are now also available from BP Resin, also based in the Czech Republic. Shown below is the company's StuG III ausf G conversion set. Many of the details are obscured here by the paint job but parts include a Topfblende mantlet and gun recuperator cylinders , late return rollers, antenna insulators, tow bracket, Notek headlight and jack in resin and many other details in photo-etched brass. Inset is the box art for the StuH 42 late version.

ROYAL MODEL

This Italian company has been producing high quality accessories and aftermarket parts since the early 1990s under the guidance of its founder, Roberto Reale. The catalogue includes complete upgrade sets in 1/35 scale for the StuG III and StuG IV. Shown below, from left toright are parts of the detail sets for the StuG III ausf G, the StuH 42 and StuG III ausf C/D.

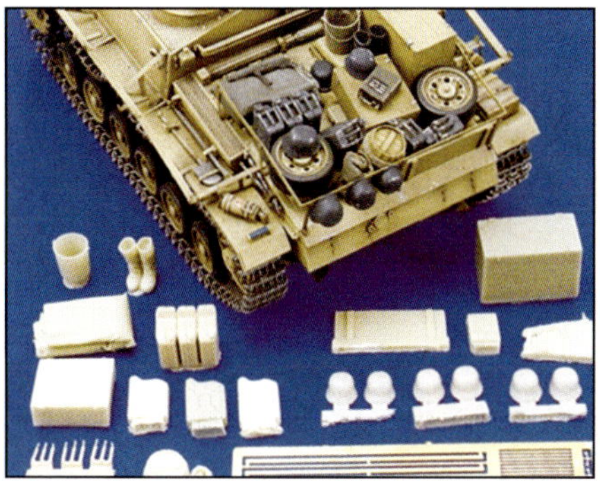

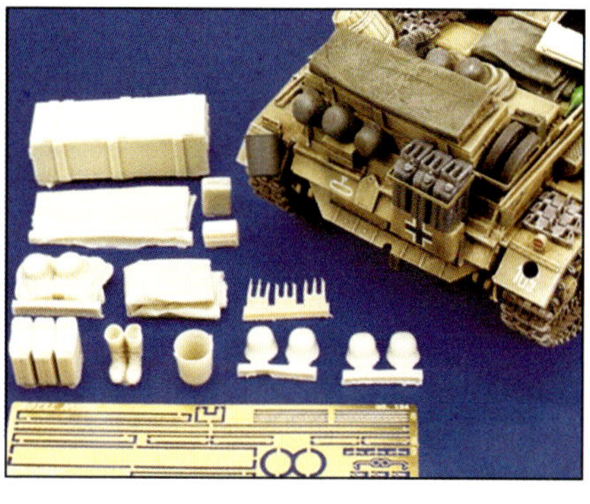

ABER

This Polish company has been manufacturing and selling upgrade sets since 1995, working in photo-etched brass, milled aluminium and brass, stainless steel and even wood. For some time now Tamiya has included Aber products with a number of their models. A full list of the accessories made specifically for the StuG III and StuG IV in all scales would be far too large to reproduce in this book and the reader can find the company's contact details on page 64. Shown here are, 1. A late pattern muzzle brake for the 7.5cm L/48 gun in 1/35 scale. 2. An early type muzzle brake and barrel in 1/35 scale for the StuG III. 3. A selection of 7.5cm projectiles, including armour-piercing and high explosive rounds, also in 1/35 scale. 4. A 1/72 scale 7.5cm muzzle brake and barrel for a StuG III. 5. A standard German fire-extinguisher and bracket in 1/16 scale. 6. An antenna insulator and antenna in 1/16 scale. These last two items would be appropriate for most German armoured vehicles.

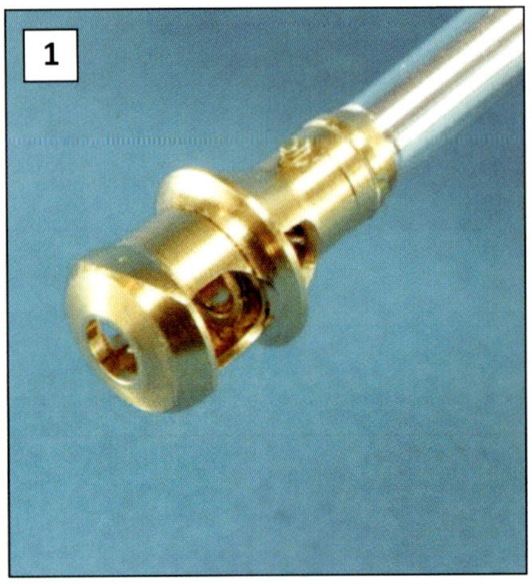

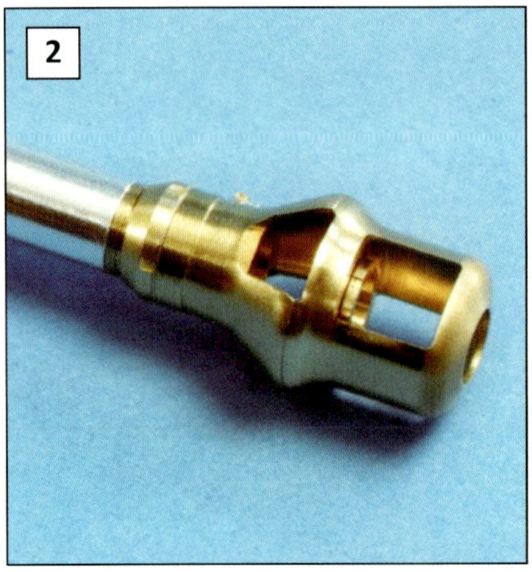

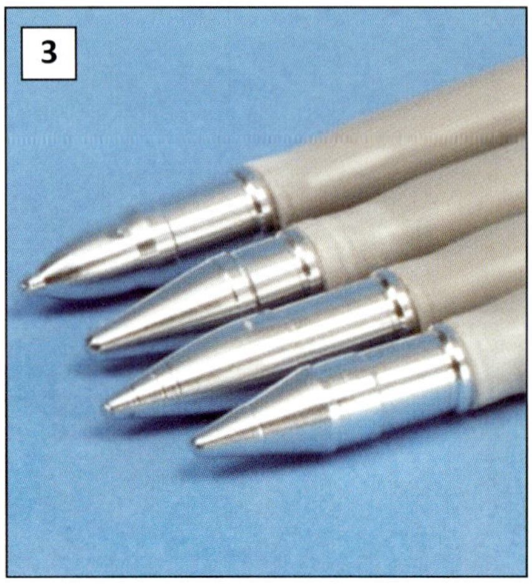

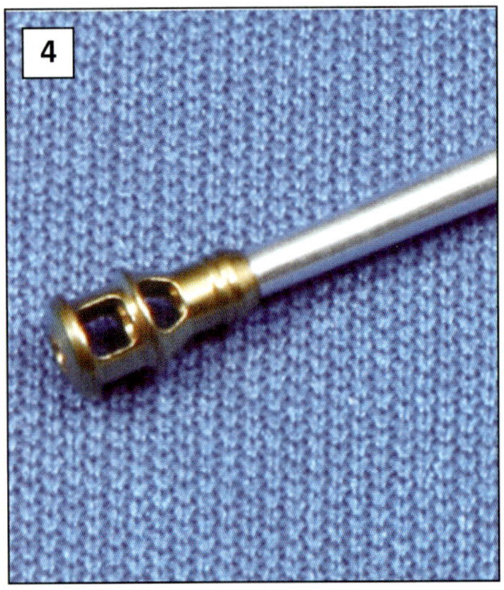

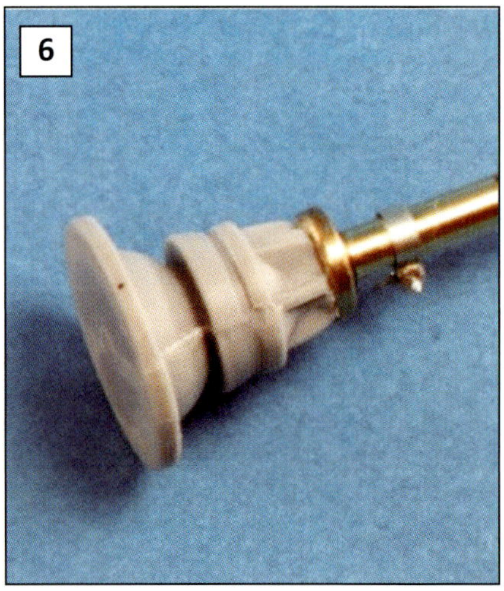

AFTERMARKET TRACKS

Most plastic kits today contain realistic tracks made from a form of vinyl which, unlike the older types, can be glued together, or hard plastic individual links. Nevertheless, there are many modellers who wish for the highest level of detail and realism possible and consequently the number of quality aftermarket products available seems to have increased in recent years, despite the extra expense and work required. Motorised models require workable tracks made up from individual links held together by pins, as were the full size items. The examples shown here, all in 1/35 scale, are 1. StuG III tracks in white metal from Russian company Master Club. 2. Early StuG III tracks in plastic from Kaizen. 3. Individual early StuG III track links in plastic from Miniart.

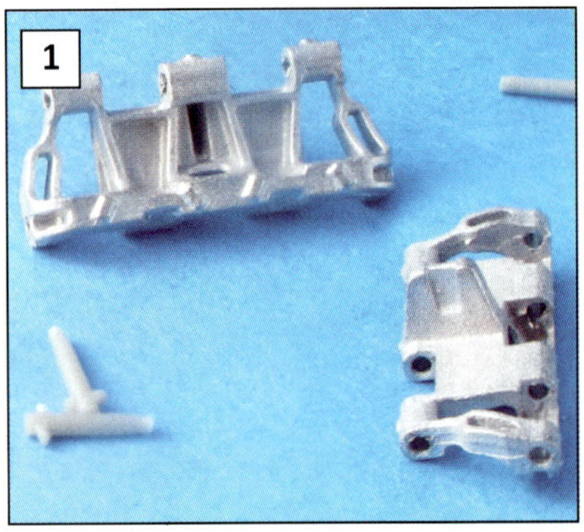

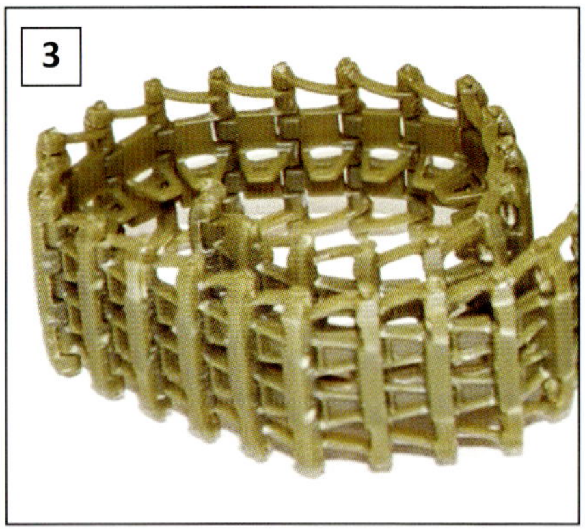

.... continued from page 16

referred to as III.Panzer-Abteilung, and in December 1944 contained thirty-seven Panther and eight Pzkpfw IV tanks with thirteen Sturmgeschütz III assault guns and a single Sturmgeschütz IV (1).

The brigade fought in the Ardennes Offensive as part of 5.Panzerarmee, most notably near Vianden and around Martelange, and was withdrawn from the front in mid-January 1945. The brigade was upgraded to a division in January 1945 and III.Panzer-Abteilung was battalion was reformed as Panzer-Regiment 101.

Führer-Begleit-Brigade. Formed at the same time as the Führer-Grenadier-Brigade, this formation's Panzerjäger-Abteilung 673 was equipped with five Sturmgeschütz III assault guns and five Sturmhaubitze 42 in December 1944 (2). The battalion was withdrawn in February 1945 to be re-equipped with the Jagdpanther but the war ended before any vehicles could be allocated.

Kampfgruppe Y. This unit was part of Panzer-Brigade 150 (Rabenhügel) and was raised specifically for the Ardennes Offensive.

It was intended that the brigade's personnel would be made up of English-speaking Germans dressed and equipped as US Army soldiers and that they would seize important road junctions and bridges by deception and generally cause confusion behind the Allied lines. In the event, very few American vehicles were available and Kampfgruppe Y was equipped with five Sturmgeschütz III assault guns disguised, rather unconvincingly, as US tank destroyers.

From late 1943, in an effort to offset the manpower shortages that the Wehrmacht was by then experiencing, a programme was instituted to increase the firepower of the army's infantry divisions and a part of this plan entailed reinforcing each division's Panzerjäger battalion with a company of ten assault guns.

This coincided with the proposed reorganisation of the Sturmgeschütze brigades to Heeres-Sturmartillerie-Brigaden and the infantry Panzerjäger companies were referred to, somewhat confusingly, as Sturmgeschütze-Abteilungen. They were usually, but not always, identified by a unique number arrived at by adding 1000 to the number of the parent formation. For example, the second company of Panzerjäger-Abteilung 176, the battalion's assault gun company, was referred to as Sturmgeschütz-Abteilung 1176. In addition a number of battalions were equipped with self-propelled anti-tank guns in place of their towed weapons but there were never enough armoured vehicles to outfit every division and those known to have operated the Sturmgeschütze III or Sturmgeschütze IV are listed below.

Panzerjäger-Abteilung 12. Formed in August 1944, the battalion was attached to 12.Volksgrenadier-Division. It took part in the fighting around Aachen and along the Roer River from September 1944 and at that time reported that ten Sturmgeschütz IV assault guns were on hand.

The battalion fought in the Ardennes, with just six of its assault guns in serviceable condition, and remained in the West until

Notes

1. Although at least one source states that a number of Jagdpanzer IV tank destroyers were on hand I am not entirely convinced that this is correct. At this time the allocation records often list these vehicles as simply 'Pz.IV' or even 'StuG.IV' causing a great deal of confusion. The assertion that the brigade had twenty-nine operational Sturmgeschütz III on hand is certainly incorrect and probably includes the vehicles of Sturmgeschütz-Brigade 911 which was attached during the Ardennes Offensive.

2. At least one source gives a figure of twenty-eight Sturmgeschütz III but this may have been the authorised strength.

Photographed in Heiderscheid in central Luxembourg on 25 December 1944, this late production vehicle is one of several assault guns lost here by III.Abteilung, Führer-Grenadier-Brigade. Note the gun travel lock and the hole in the upper left corner of the gun mantlet for a coaxial machine gun which was fitted from October 1944.

April 1945 when it was destroyed in the Ruhr Pocket battles. In keeping with established practice the battalion's assault gun company was referred to as Sturmgeschütz-Abteilung 1012.

Panzerjäger-Abteilung 36. Formed in October 1944 and attached to 36. Volksgrenadier-Division, the battalion was equipped with ten Sturmgeschütz IV assault guns, all concentrated in its second company which was referred to as Sturmgeschütz-Abteilung 1036.

The division took part in Operation Nordwind in January 1945 and although the infantry element was the equivalent of not much more than a strong regiment, and the Panzerjäger battalion had just over half its authorised assault guns, some gains were made before the attack was called off. In April 1945 the last the remnants of 36.Volksgrenadier-Division withdrew into Upper Bavaria where they eventually surrendered to the Americans.

Panzerjäger-Abteilung 119. Formed in August 1944 for 19.Grenadier-Division, by October the battalion's second company was equipped with ten assault guns and referred to, in some sources, as Sturmgeschütz-Abteilung 1119 (1).

By that time the division had been renamed 19.Volksgrenadier-Division and sent to the front where it served in the Saarpfalz region, supporting 21.Panzer-Division and 17.SS-Panzergrenadier-Division.

In January 1945, at the conclusion of Operation Nordwind, the battalion reported that three Sturmgeschütz IV assault guns were available for deployment. In late March 1945, 19.Volksgrenadier-Division, by this time reduced to a weak Kampfgruppe, was disbanded with the survivors reinforcing other units, mainly 2.Gebirgs-Division.

Panzerjäger-Abteilung 176. Formed in October 1944 as Panzerjäger-Abteilung 1176, the battalion was attached to 176.Infanterie-Division. The battalion was never to receive its full allocation, reporting that six Sturmgeschütz III assault guns were on hand at the beginning of November, while just one vehicle was considered combat-ready in December.

In April 1945 the battalion was renamed Panzerjäger-Abteilung 176.

Panzerjäger-Abteilung 184. Formed in February 1944 as a single anti-tank company and attached to 84.Infanterie-Division. Although the battalion was expanded in the following April it was completely destroyed in the battles around Falaise which marked the end of the Normandy campaign. Subsequently rebuilt as a single company and renamed Panzerjäger-Kompanie 1184, just two Sturmgeschütz III assault guns were on hand in January 1945 when the division was fighting against the British around Kleve as part of 1.Fallschirm-Armee.

Panzerjäger-Abteilung 185. Attached to 185.Infanterie-Division, the battalion's Panzerjäger-Kompanie 1185 was equipped with just two Sturmgeschütz III assault guns in January 1945. In the following April the company was incorporated into Infanterie-Division Potsdam as Panzerjäger-Abteilung 185.

Panzerjäger-Abteilung 212. Attached to 221.Volksgrenadier-Division, the battalion was allocated a total of five Sturmgeschütz III assault guns although just three of these took part in the initial actions of Operation Wacht am Rhein, the Ardennes Offensive, in mid-December 1944. Remnants of the division were able to reach Baumholder in Bavaria where they surrendered to units of the US Army in May 1945. The battalion's assault gun company was referred to as Sturmgeschütz-Abteilung 1212.

Panzerjäger-Abteilung 235. Attached to 198.Infanterie-Division, the battalion was issued with four Sturmgeschütz III assault guns in December 1944 and was reinforced with the remnants of Sturmgeschütz-Kompanie 2111 in the first weeks of 1945. The battalion's assault gun company received ten Jagdpanzer 38t Hetzer tank destroyers in April 1945 and was probably renamed at this time to Jagdpanzer-Kompanie 1235.

Panzerjäger-Abteilung 243. Attached to 243.Infanterie-Division which had been stationed in the Contentin Peninsula when the Normandy invasion began, the battalion's first company was equipped with a number of Marder self-propelled anti-tank guns while 2.Kompanie, referred to as Sturmgeschütz-Abteilung 1243, had ten Sturmgeschütz III assault guns. The battalion was almost wiped out in the Normandy battles and the survivors were used to build Panzerjäger-Abteilung 1176.

Panzerjäger-Abteilung 245. Little is known of this unit other than that it was formed in July with three companies for 245.Infanterie-Division.

There is a record of the battalion receiving fourteen Jadgpanzer 38t Hetzer tank destroyers some time in December 1944 but four Sturmgeschütz III assault guns were still on hand in January 1945 and these may have supported Grenadier-Regiment 935 and Grenadier-Regiment 937 in an attack on British positions around Witzeeze, east of Hamburg near the Elbe-Lübeck canal, during the night of 30 April 1945. Very late in the war it seems that the battalion's assault gun company was renamed Jagdpanzer-Kompanie 1245.

Panzerjäger-Abteilung 256. Attached to 256.Volksgrenadier-Division, this battalion, like many units of the later war divisions, never received its full allocation

Notes

1. The OKW situation maps for December 1944 and January 1945 clearly show a notation for 'St.G.A.1119' quite separate from the parent division. Most written accounts simply refer to this unit as the battalion's second company.

of armoured vehicles, reporting that just four Sturmgeschütz III assault guns were on hand in December 1944 and it is quite possible that these all were received in that month. The division took part in Operation Nordwind, capturing the high ground north of Lichtenberg, between Bitche and Strasbourg, but suffering excessively heavy casualties in the process.

In mid-April 1945, the last remnants of the division were thrown into the fighting around Chemnitz, near the present-day border with the Czech Republic, where most perished.

Panzerjäger-Abteilung 276. Originally formed in January 1944 from the staff of Panzerjäger-Abteilung 138 and a single anti-tank company, the battalion was destroyed during the fighting in Normandy.

Rebuilt in September 1944 with three companies and subordinated to 276.Volksgrenadier-Division the battalion reported that ten Sturmgeschütz IV were on hand in November. The battalion's assault gun company was referred to as Sturmgeschütz-Abteilung 1276.

The division took part in the Ardennes Offensive and was later wiped out in the fighting south of Remagen in March 1945.

Panzerjäger-Abteilung 326. Formed in January 1944, and attached to 326.Infanterie-Division, the battalion reported that ten Sturmgeschütz III assault guns and fourteen Marder III self-propelled anti-tank guns were on hand in July. The division was destroyed in the Normandy battles and rebuilt as 326.Volksgrenadier-Division.

The Panzerjäger battalion's second company received fourteen Jagdpanzer 38t Hetzer tank destroyers in November 1944 and was probably renamed at this time as Sturmgeschütz-Abteilung 1326. Of the six Sturmgeschütz III available in November, a single vehicle is reported as being on hand in the following month and it is likely that this had been lost by the start of the Ardennes Offensive.

Panzerjäger-Abteilung 331. Formed in February 1944, and attached to 331.Infanterie-Division, the battalion's second, or assault gun, company was known as Sturmgeschütz-Abteilung 1331 and was equipped with ten Sturmgeschütz IV assault guns.

The battalion fought in Normandy and was completely destroyed after being trapped in the Falaise Pocket, the last assault guns being destroyed by their own crews during the evening of 17 August 1944.

Panzerjäger-Abteilung 340. Formed in September 1944 from the remnants of Panzerjäger-Abteilung 377 and attached to 340.Volksgrenadier-Division, the battalion reported that fourteen Jagdpanzer 38t Hetzer tank destroyers and ten Sturmgeschütz IV assault guns were on hand at the beginning of December 1944. The division was never fully formed and took part in the Ardennes Offensive with Kampfgruppe Tolsdorff supporting the attacks of 12.SS-Panzer-Division.

In March 1945 the survivors were absorbed by 19.Volksgrenadier-Division. The battalion's assault gun company was referred to as Sturmgeschütz-Abteilung 1340.

Panzerjäger-Abteilung 346. Attached to 346.Infanterie-Division, the battalion's second company was referred to as Sturmgeschütz-Abteilung 1346. In June 1944 the battalion reported that ten Sturmgeschütz III assault guns were on hand during the fighting in Normandy where Oberleutnant Franz Ludwig, the commander of 2.Kompanie, was famously credited with the destruction of at least sixteen Allied tanks.

With the rest of 346.Infanterie-Division the battalion was almost completely destroyed in August 1944, losing many of its men including Oberleutnant Ludwig, and was rebuilt in the following December. The battalion remained in Holland for the remainder of the war, surrendering to the British in May 1945.

By the end of the war 2.Kompanie had been reduced to three assault guns, of which one was an early model with the short 7.5cm gun, a single Marder III and a Bergepanzer III (1).

Panzerjäger-Abteilung 348. Formed in January 1943 and attached to 348.Infanterie-Division, the battalion's second company was referred to as Sturmgeschütz-Abteilung 1348 and in mid-1944 was equipped with ten Sturmgeschütz III assault guns. When the division was destroyed in August 1944 the battalion operated semi-independently and was for some time subordinated to 3.Fallschirmjager-Division.

In February 1945 the battalion was disbanded and used to create Panzerjäger-Abteilung 190.

Panzerjäger-Abteilung 352. Formed in November 1943 with a self-propelled company, a Flak company and an assault gun company, the latter referred to as Sturmgeschütz-Abteilung 1352, the battalion was equipped with ten Sturmgeschütz III assault guns and fourteen Marder III self-propelled anti-tank guns in June 1944. The battalion was completely wiped out in the fighting in Normandy and rebuilt in September 1944 with four companies from the remnants of Panzerjäger-Abteilung 1581 receiving ten Jagdpanzer 38t Hetzers in the following

.... *continued on page 53*

Notes

1. It is possible that at sometime in April 1945 the battalion's 3.Kompanie acquired the Pzkpfw III ausf N tanks of Panzer-Kompanie 224 but this has not been confirmed.

PANZERJÄGER-ABTEILUNG, VOLKSGRENADIER-DIVISION, 1944

As mentioned in the main text, from late 1943 the Oberkommando der Wehrmacht (OKW), faced with mounting personnel losses, embarked on a programme to expand the overall firepower of the army's infantry divisions. In addition to an increase in the number of automatic weapons available to infantry formations, it was intended that each division's Panzerjäger battalion be allocated a company of ten or fourteen assault guns. The establishment shown here was specifically created for a Volksgrenadier-Division, the first of which were raised in the autumn of 1944, but it is similar to those of Infanterie, Grenadier and Gebirgs divisions. The Panzerjäger battalion's assault gun company was referred to as a Sturmgeschütz-Abteilung and uniquely numbered within the division by adding 1000 to the division's number. For example, the assault gun company of 559.Volksgrenadier-Division was referred to as Sturmgeschütz-Abteilung 1559. There were, of course, exceptions to this rule and they are mentioned in the unit histories.

Stab und Stabskompanie
einer Panzerjägerabteilung (gemischte)
KStN 1106 von 1.2.1944

Stab

Stabsbatterie

Nachrichten-Zug
Signal Platoon

Instandsetzungs-Staffel (kfz und Waffen)
Maintenance Section (vehicles and weapons)

Gefechtstross
Ammunition Section

Abteilungsverpflegungstross
Ration Section

Gepäckstross
Baggage Section

schwere Panzerjägerkompanie
(mot Z) (freie Gliederung)
KStN 1140 (fG) von 1.4.1944

Gruppe Führer
1st Company Commander

The company's three platoons could be equipped with either 3 x 7.5cm PaK 97/38, 3 x 7.5cm PaK 40 or 3 x 7.62cm PaK 36. The latter were conversions of captured Russian anti-tank weapons. The guns were towed by SdKfz 3 or SdKfz 11 halftracks or RSO 3-ton fully-tracked vehicles. An Ausführung B version of the KStN allowed for four gun platoons.

Sturmgeschützabteilung
(in Panzerjäger-Abteilung)
(10 oder 14 Geschützen)
KStN 1149 von 1.2.1944

Gruppe Führer
2nd Company Commander

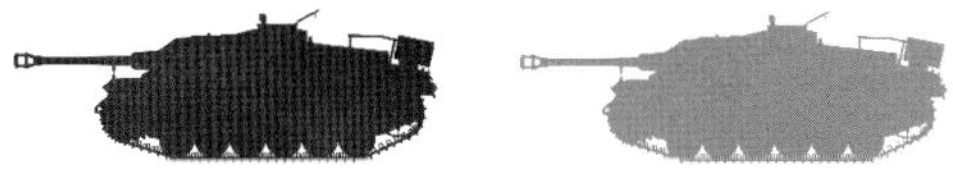
StuG III | StuG III

1.Zug

StuG III | StuG III | StuG III | StuG III

or

1.Zug

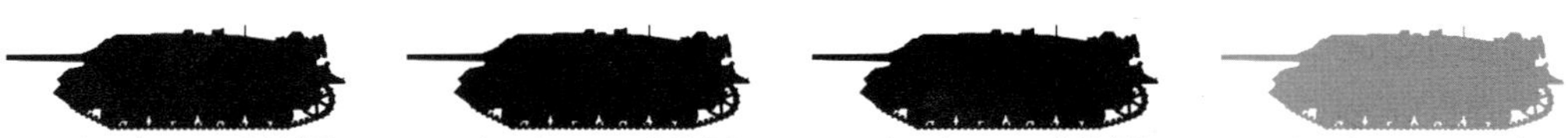
Jagdpanzer IV L/48 | Jagdpanzer IV L/48 | Jagdpanzer IV L/48 | Jagdpanzer IV L/48

or

1.Zug

Jagdpanzer 38(t) | Jagdpanzer 38(t) | Jagdpanzer 38(t) | Jagdpanzer 38(t)

2.Zug
As for 1.Zug

3.Zug
As for 1.Zug

The vehicles shown here in a lighter shade are appropriate only for the Ausführung B version of this KStN which allowed for four-gun platoons, giving an overall total of fourteen. In the official order the ten-gun company was referred to as Ausführung A. The type of vehicle would have be consistent throughout the company, including the headquarters.

Fliegerabwehrkompanie (zu 9 Geschützen 3.7 cm Flak) (mot Z)
oder
Fliegerabwehrkompanie (zu 3.7 cm Flakzwilling) (mot Z)
KStN 198 von 1.4.1944

Gruppe Führer
3rd Company Commander

1.Zug

3 x 3.7cm Flak anti-aircraft guns with Sd.Ah 52 or Sd.Ah 58 trailer, towed by an SdKfz 3 Maultier 4.5-ton halftrack with one 3-ton truck for ammunition and spares

or

1.Zug

3 x 3.7cm Flakzwilling anti-aircraft guns with Sd.Ah 52 or Sd.Ah 58 trailer, towed by an SdKfz 3 Maultier 4.5-ton halftrack with one 3-ton truck for ammunition and spares

2.Zug
As for 1.Zug

3.Zug
As for 1.Zug

.... continued from page 51

November. As part of 352.Volksgrenadier-Division the battalion took part in the Ardennes Offensive with just six serviceable tank destroyers and was reduced to little more that a weak Kampfgruppe by early 1945.

Panzerjäger-Abteilung 353. Formed in February 1944 and attached to 353.Infanterie-Division, the battalion was equipped with fourteen Marder III self-propelled anti-tank guns with the first company, ten Sturmgeschütz III assault guns with the second and a number of 3.7cm anti-aircraft guns mounted on Sdkfz 7 halftracks in the third. The battalion's assault gun company was referred to as Sturmgeschütz-Abteilung 1353.

Almost completely destroyed in the Normandy battles, the battalion was rebuilt in November 1944 with ten Sturmgeschütz IV vehicles. In January 1945 the battalion was transferred to 719.Infanterie-Division and ended the war fighting in the Saarpfalz region.

Panzerjäger-Abteilung 361. Attached to 361.Volksgrenadier-Division, the battalion reported that ten Sturmgeschütz IV assault guns were on hand in October 1944.

After just five weeks of training the battalion was involved in the fighting in Lorraine and the Vosges in November and December 1944 and took part in Operation Nordwind during the first weeks of 1945. At that time the battalion received two Sturmgeschütz III assault guns and these may have been the only armoured vehicles on hand. The division was disbanded in the following February after suffering heavy casualties.

Panzerjäger-Abteilung 553. Attached to 553.Grenadier-Division, the battalion took part in the fighting for the fortress city of Metz in September 1944 when it was equipped with ten Sturmgeschütz III assault guns. In December, after the battles along the Moselle River, the battalion reported that five of the assault guns were still serviceable and that a single Marder II and two Marder III self-propelled anti-tank guns were also on hand.

Reformed in February 1945, the battalion was equipped with ten Hetzer tank destroyers and may have been made up of just one company. The rebuilt battalion was initially referred to as Panzerjäger-Abteilung 1553 but within less than a month had reverted to its old title.

Panzerjäger-Abteilung 712. Attached to 712. Infanterie-Division, the battalion received ten Sturmgeschütz III assault guns in November 1944. After fighting in the Netherlands the division was transferred to the East in January 1945.

Although no definitive identification is possible, this Sturmgeschütz III ausf G may be one of the ten assault guns on hand with Sturmgeschütz-Abteiling 1553, which was operating near the town of Sittard in southern Holland in mid-Septembr 1944, close to where this photograph would have been taken. Another, perhaps more likely, candidate is Sturmgeschütz-Brigade 394 which was supporting 12.Infanterie-Division here against units of the US 30th Division. Note the many kill rings on the barrel.

A Sturmgeschütz III ausf B of Minenkommando Dänemark, probably photographed in 1946. This unit's only other assault gun was a Sturmgeschütz III ausf G which was almost certainly manufactured before June 1944 when the travel lock was introduced into production. At some point the main gun was removed from this later model vehicle but at least one photograph exists were the gun is in place. Note that the Sturmgeschütz shown here is fitted with hull Schürzen and has a very comprehensive coat of Zimmerit.

Panzerjäger-Abteilung 1089. Formed in October 1944 from the remnants of Sturmgeschütz-Kompanie 2112, which had been part of Panzer-Brigade 112, the battalion reported that five Sturmgeschütz III assault guns were on hand in December 1944.

Attached to 189.Volksgrenadier-Division, the battalion was referred to in official documentation as Panzer-Jagd-Kompanie (Sturmgeschütz) 1089 and it is likely that its strength was never more than that of a weak company. The division was almost totally destroyed in the fighting in Alsace in February 1945 and although an attempt was made to rebuild it, the process was abandoned in early April. The Panzerjäger company received ten Jagdpanzer 38t Hetzers before it was disbanded.

Panzerjäger-Abteilung 1553. See Panzerjäger-Abteilung 553 on page 53.

Panzerjäger-Abteilung 1559. Formed as a single company in August 1944 and attached to 559.Volksgrenadier-Division, by the following December the battalion had been expanded to a Panzerjäger company, a Flak company and an assault gun company which was referred to as Sturmgeschütz-Abteilung 1559. In January 1945, when the division was fighting in defence of the Westwall fortifications, the battalion reported that ten Sturmgeschütz III assault guns were available for deployment. This unit should not be confused with schwere Panzerjäger-Abteilung 559.

Panzerjäger-Kompanie 1184. See Panzerjäger-Abteilung 184 on page 50.

Panzerjäger-Kompanie 1185. See Panzerjäger-Abteilung 185 above.

Panzerjäger-Kompanie 1338. This unit had been part of Schnelle-Abteilung 338 of 338.Infanterie-Division until that formation was disbanded in October 1944. The battalion's Füsilier, Flak and Panzerjäger companies were then supposed to have operated as independent units, but there is evidence that Panzerjäger-Kompanie 1338 was with the rebuilt division when it was destroyed in the Ruhr Pocket in April 1945. Earlier, in January, the company reported that ten Sturmgeschütz III assault guns were on hand.

Minenkommando Dänemark. Although strictly speaking this company-sized formation was not part of the German armed forces, it deserves some mention. Formed by the Allies after 1945 from prisoners of war, Minenkommando Dänemark was tasked with removing the more than 1,000,000 mines laid along the Danish coast that had made up part of the Atlantik Wall defences. The company was equipped with two Sturmgeschütz III assault guns taken over from Panzer-Ersatz und Lehr-Abteilung 400, a number of Pzkpfw III tanks and several halftracks. The fully-tracked vehicles were originally fitted with concrete rollers but when they were found to be ineffective, steel versions were produced.

Although the German personnel were for the most part volunteers, the use of prisoners in such a dangerous operation was strongly objected to by the International Red Cross (1).

Notes

1. The use of prisoners of war in mine clearing actions is strictly prohibited under the terms of the Geneva Convention and over 300 German servicemen were killed or seriously wounded in these operations.

Above: A Sturmgeschütz III ausf G of SS-Sturmgeschütz-Abteilung 1 photographed in Normandy. The unit insignia of 1.SS-Panzer-Division is just visible of the right-hand side fender. The foliage camouflage was a common sight in Normandy where the Allies enjoyed almost complete air superiority. The so-called waffle pattern of Zimmerit application, which many of this battalion's guns seem to have had, was indicative of vehicles manufactured by Alkett.

The Sturmgeschütz III was the first fully-tracked armoured vehicle to serve with the Waffen-SS when a battery of six guns was formed for Leibstandarte SS Adolf Hitler (mot) as Panzer-Sturm-Batterie LSSAH in May 1940. In February 1942 the battery was increased to a full battalion of three batteries and a staff element and renamed Sturmgeschütz-Abteilung LSSAH.

On 22 October 1943 the battalion was again renamed as SS-Sturmgeschütz-Abteilung 1 and the total number of guns was increased to thirty-five.

Assault gun battalions were planned for a number of Waffen-SS divisions but many were either incorporated into the Panzer regiments or Panzerjäger battalions or simply never formed, as in the case of 12.SS-Panzer-Division Hitler Jugend. The units that took part in the battles in western Europe during 1944 and 1945 are listed below.

SS-Sturmgeschütz-Abteilung 1. Formed in October 1943 the battalion was attached to 1.SS-Panzer-Division Leibstandarte SS Adolf Hitler and reported that forty-five Sturmgeschütz III assault guns were on hand in July 1944. The battalion fought in the Normandy battles, going into action for the first time at Louvigny on 10 July in support of the division's Panzer regiment. After the fighting around Rennes in early August the guns of the battalion were dispersed to several Kampfgruppen and this arrangement continued for the remainder of the campaign. A single assault gun survived the battles at Falaise and the retreat to the Seine and the remnants of the battalion were absorbed by SS-Panzerjäger-Abteilung 1 and re-equipped with Jagdpanzer IV tank destroyers in November 1944.

SS-Sturmgeschütz-Abteilung 2. Attached to 2.SS-Panzer-Division Das Reich, the battalion fought in Normandy, reporting that forty-five Sturmgeschütz III assault guns were on hand in July 1944. By 6 August, the day before the Mortain counterattack commenced, the battalion had been reduced to eight serviceable machines.

The battalion was largely destroyed in the Normandy battles and on 8 September 1944 the survivors were used to rebuild SS-Panzerjäger-Abteilung 2 and equipped with two companies of Jagdpanzer IV tank destroyers and a company of towed 7.5cm guns.

SS-Panzer-Regiment 2. Attached to 2.SS-Panzer-Division, the regiment took part in the Normandy battles where it was almost completely wiped out.

Rebuilt in November 1944, the regiment was made up of I.Abteilung, equipped with fifty-eight Panthers, and II.Abteilung organised as a mixed battalion made up of two companies, each with fourteen Sturmgeschütz III assault guns, and two companies of Pzkpfw IV tanks.

The division took part in the Ardennes Offensive, forming part of the 5.Panzerarmee reserve with 9.SS-Panzer-Division, and was withdrawn from the front in mid-January 1945. In late February the rebuilt 2.SS-Panzer-Division was transferred to the East.

SS-Panzer-Regiment 9. Attached to 9.SS Panzer Division Hohenstaufen, the regiment was transferred to France from the Eastern Front in mid-June 1944 and at that time II.Abteilung had a total of forty Sturmgeschütz III assault guns with 7.Kompanie and 8.Kompanie while the other companies were equipped with Pzkpfw IV tanks. The Panthers of the regiment's I.Abteilung had been in training at Truppenübungsplatz Mailly-le-Camp, south of Reims, for some time and later joined the regiment in Normandy.

The division remained in the area south of Caen until 16 August 1944, when it was ordered to withdraw towards Vimoutier, and with the last tanks of 2.SS Panzer Division, was involved in the attempts to relieve the German units encircled near Falaise.

Following the battles in Normandy the remaining armoured vehicles were handed over to Panzer-Regiment 15 of 11.Panzer-Division.

Parts of the division famously took part in the defence of Arnhem but did not possess any assault guns at this time, although Panzerjäger-Abteilung 9 had two Jagdpanzer IV tank destroyers.

The regiment was rebuilt in November 1944 with I.Abteilung fully equipped with Panthers and II.Abteilung organised as a mixed battalion made up of two companies, each with fourteen Sturmgeschütz III assault guns, and two full companies of Pzkpfw IV tanks. The division took part in the Ardennes Offensive as part of 6.Panzerarmee and at the end of January 1945 was withdrawn from the front to rest and refit.

In February, 9.SS-Panzer-Division was sent to the East and was engaged in Operation Spring Awakening, the last major German offensive of the war. On 1 May 1945 a large part of the division, which had managed to make its way to the West, surrendered to the Americans.

The Sturmgeschütz battalion raised for this division in 1943 was incorporated into the Panzerjäger-Abteilung in June 1944 and equipped with Jagdpanzer IV tank destroyers.

SS-Panzer-Regiment 10. Attached to 10.SS-Panzer-Division Frundsberg, in June 1944 the regiment's II.Abteilung was made up of thirty-nine Pzkpfw IV tanks and thirty-eight Sturmgeschütz III assault guns, including vehicles under repair (1).

Most of the regiment's vehicles and heavy equipment were lost in Normandy but some sources state that at least four assault guns were still on hand during the defence of Arnhem in September 1944.

Photographed near Tournai-sur-Dive, north-east of Trun, at the conclusion of the Falaise battles on 21 August 1944, this Sturmgeschütz III ausf G is one of the forty assault guns on hand with II.Abteilung, SS-Panzer-Regiment 9 when the campaign began. In the original print of this image it is possible to see a version of the unit insignia of 9.SS-Panzer-Division Hohenstaufen (inset) on the right front fender. The absence of a gun travel lock on the hull front would suggest that this vehicle was assembled prior to May 1944.

Notes

1. The regiment's I.Abteilung was training in France at this time and not join the division until 1945. The Panzerjäger Abteilung was still being formed and would take no part in the Normandy fighting.

Although a notation on this photograph states that the location here is Normandy, the complete lack of Zimmerit would suggest that the date is much later than June or July 1944. The company number certainly suggests SS-Panzer-Abteilung 17, the only unit in the West with a first company equipped with these vehicles, and it is tempting to speculate that this may be one of the late August consignment that was thought to have gone missing.

In November the regiment was rebuilt with just one battalion made up of two companies of Panthers and two companies of Pzkpfw IV tanks. The Sturmgeschütz battalion that was raised for 10.SS-Panzer-Division in February 1943 was disbanded and the personnel and equipment were absorbed by the division's Panzer regiment, forming the seventh and eighth companies.

SS-Panzer-Abteilung 17. Attached to 17.SS Panzergrenadier-Division Götz von Berlichingen, the battalion had forty-two Sturmgeschütz IV assault guns on hand in June 1944 when the Allied landings in Normandy began. The battalion staff had no armoured vehicles at this time and would have to wait until mid-August when three Panzerbefehlswagen IV command tanks arrived.

The battalion took part in the battles in Normandy, in particular at Carentan against elements of the US 101st Airborne Division and at Coutances where most of the heavy equipment was lost. By the time of the Mortain counterattack the remnants of the division were formed into two Kampfgruppen under the command of 2.SS-Panzer-Division and the five surviving assault guns had all been sent to the greater Paris area for repairs and it is unclear if they were ever returned.

In late August a total of seventeen new Sturmgeschütz III guns were allocated to the battalion but these may never have arrived as the division reported on 15 September 1944 that just five serviceable Sturmgeschütz of an unspecified type were available (1). In November 1944 the division was rebuilt and a total of nineteen Sturmgeschütz IV were issued, followed in December by forty Sturmgeschütz III and four Flakpanzer IV vehicles. It is probably safe to assume that the Sturmgeschütz IV all went to SS-Panzer-Abteilung 17 while the majority of the Sturmgeschütz III were allocated to the division's Panzerjäger battalion which later reported twenty-nine of these vehicles on hand (see below).The division took part in Operation Nordwind and at the end of January 1945 reported that forty-two assault guns were on hand. The division was engaged in the battles for the Westwall and the defence of Nuremberg although the last of the armoured vehicles had been abandoned on 22 March 1945 (2).

SS-Panzerjäger-Abteilung 17. The battalion took part in the fighting in Normandy equipped with Marder III self-propelled anti-tank guns, both the 7.62cm and 7.5cm armed versions, and these were later joined by two companies of Jagdpanzer IV tank destroyers.

By the beginning of August 1944 just five of the Jagdpanzer IV remained and the battalion was withdrawn and rebuilt. At the conclusion of Operation Nordwind the battalion reported that second and third companies could field twenty-nine assault guns, probably Sturmgeschütz III, while the third company had a single Marder III and a number of towed anti-tank guns. The staff element was equipped with two Jagdpanzer IV tank destroyers.

Elements of the division were fighting in isolated Kampfgruppen as late as 5 May 1945.

Notes

1. Confusingly, the term Sturmgeschütz was often used to describe any type of tank destroyer in official reports.
2. This may have included as many as sixty-two assault guns, of which forty-seven were serviceable, and two of the Panzerbefehlswagen tanks. These numbers are, however, difficult to reconcile with the figures given for January which are certainly correct. Units of the Waffen-SS were notorious for under-reporting their strength.

In January 1944 orders issued by Oberkommando der Wehrmacht (OKW) and Oberkommando der Luftwaffe (OKL) directed that an assault gun brigade should be raised for each of the Fallschirmjäger corps then in existence.

The brigades were made up of three batteries of ten guns with an additional gun for the brigade commander, giving a total of thirty-one. Although every effort was made to recruit the assault gun crews from parachute infantry units, most came from Flak formations and it seems that neither of the brigades operated with their authorised strength.

Fallschirm-Sturmgeschütz-Brigade 11. First raised in January 1944 as Sturmgeschütz-Abteilung 1 der Luftwaffe, this battalion was very quickly renamed Sturmgeschütz-Brigade 1 der Luftwaffe in April 1944 and finally Fallschirm-Sturmgeschütz-Brigade 11 in the following June. At that time the battalion was at full strength with twenty-two Sturmgeschütz III assault guns and nine Sturmhaubitze 42 on hand. The battalion fought in Normandy where it was almost completely destroyed and was rebuilt in November 1944.

Subordinated to 5.Fallschirmjäger-Division, the battalion took part in the Ardennes Offensive and was badly mauled when the assault guns came up against the tanks of US 4th Armoured Division. Withdrawn to Germany the battalion was again rebuilt and, after a brief sojourn in the East, was once again attached to 5.Fallschirmjäger-Division, taking part in the fighting around Cologne in March 1945. At the same time the battalion was renamed Fallschirm-Sturmgeschütz-Brigade 111.

Fallschirm-Sturmgeschütz-Brigade 12. Originally formed in January 1944 with four batteries and named Sturmgeschütz-Abteilung 2 der Luftwaffe, the battalion was renamed Sturmgeschütz-Brigade 2 der Luftwaffe in March. By June, when the battalion was committed to the fighting in Normandy, the name had been changed to Fallschirm-Sturmgeschütz-Brigade 12 and the number of batteries reduced to three. The battalion was almost completely wiped out in the Falaise battles, reporting that a single Sturmhaubitze 42 was available in August 1944. Rebuilt in September, the battalion took part in the fighting around Arnhem after which it was withdrawn to Germany.

Rebuilt once again, the battalion returned to the front in February 1945 and supported 7.Fallschirmjäger-Division, with perhaps as few as five assault guns, during the battles in the Reichswald. In a single month, between 24 March and 24 April 1945, Leutnant Heinz Deutsch, the

At left: Two crewmen of a Luftwaffe Sturmhaubitze 42, with the large muzzle brake visible in the background, photographed in Normandy during the summer of 1944. Below: A Sturmgeschütz III ausf G of Fallschirm-Sturmgeschütz-Brigade 12 in France just prior to the Allied invasion. Below, left: The Luftwaffe Ground Assault Badge instituted in March 1942 and awarded in its lowest grade for participation in three separate actions. As the war progressed versions recognising 25, 50, 75 and 100 engagements were introduced.

One of the five Sturmgeschütz III ausf G assault guns of Panzer-Brigade 150 which were disguised to resemble US Army tank destroyers as mentioned in the text. All were painted in a green shade, presumably RAL 6003 Olivgrün, and marked with white recognition stars as shown here.

commander of the third battery, was credited with the destruction of forty-six Allied tanks and became the only member of a Luftwaffe assault gun unit to receive the Ritterkreuz.

On 28 March 1945 the battalion was renamed Fallschirm-Sturmgeschütz-Brigade 121.

In early 1942 a number of infantry divisions were raised from surplus Luftwaffe personnel and referred to as Luftwaffen-Felddivisionen. Most of these were employed on the Russian Front and by November 1943 all had been incorporated into the army and renamed Feld-Divisionen (L), the suffix being the only reminder of their origins.

Although they were, strictly speaking, units of the Heer, I have included them here. Those units which fought in the West are listed below.

Panzerjäger-Abteilung 16 (L). Attached to 16.Feld-Division (L), the battalion was equipped with ten Sturmgeschütz III assault guns in July 1944. The division was so badly mauled in the Normandy battles that it was dissolved in August 1944 with the remnants eventually going to the newly-formed 16.Volksgrenadier-Division. The second, or assault gun, company of the battalion was referred to as Sturmgeschütz -Abteilung 1016 (L).

Panzerjäger-Abteilung 17(L). Attached to 17.Feld-Division (L), the battalion was not involved in the Normandy battles but took part in the defence of Paris under the command of 5.Panzerarmee. The division was disbanded in September 1944 with the Panzerjäger battalion reporting that eight Sturmgeschütz III assault guns were on hand at that time. The survivors were used to form 167.Volksgrenadier-Division.

Panzerjäger-Abteilung 18(L). Attached to 18.Feld-Division (L), the battalion reported that seven Sturmgeschütz III assault guns were on hand with its 2.Kompanie in August 1944. In the same month the division was destroyed in the fighting around Mons and the few survivors were incorporated into 18.Volksgrenadier-Division. The assault gun company was referred to as Sturmgeschütz-Abteilung 1018 (L).

Fallschirm-Ersatz und Ausbildungs-Regiment Hermann Göring. Composed of an infantry battalion, a mixed infantry and Panzer battalion and a mixed artillery and anti-aircraft battalion, the regiment reported that a single Sturmgeschütz III was on hand in January 1945. Later that month the regiment was transferred to the Eastern Front and completely destroyed in the battles for Graudenz, modern-day Gradziadz in Poland.

The principal manufacturers of the Sturmgeschütz III were the firms of Alkett of Berlin-Borsigwarde, Mühlenbau und Industrie Aktiengesellschaft (MIAG) of Brunswick and Maschinenfabrik Augsburg-Nürnberg (MAN) at their Nuremberg plant. Various components, such as the main gun and optics, were developed and produced by other concerns but the three companies mentioned above provided the fully assembled vehicles (1).

The major production version of the Sturmgeschütz III encountered during the period covered by this book was the ausf G model of which over 8,000 examples were assembled between December 1942 and April 1945.

As this version far outnumbered all the earlier variants combined, and is also the most relevant to our study, I have mainly restricted the modifications listed below to the Sturmgeschütz III ausf G. Many of the earlier models did soldier on until the end of the war and various technical aspects and identifying features of those vehicles are shown and discussed in the Camouflage & Markings section, which begins on page 17, and in the photographs that are included with the main text.

The sole manufacturer of what came to be known as the Sturmgeschütz IV was the firm of Friedrich Krupp AG and all work was carried out at the company's Magdeburg plant and the reasons for this are discussed on page 2.

Assembly was undertaken side by side with the Pzkfpw IV and consequently the production changes listed here for the Sturmgeschütz IV are largely assumed and are based on those relevant to the Pzkfpw IV ausf J and the available photographic evidence. It is quite possible however that a number of those changes were made at some later date or never at all.

Further, modifications made to the Sturmgeschütz III were also incorporated into the Sturmgeschütz IV.

It should also be noted that when earlier models of both types of assault gun were returned to Germany for major repairs many of the latest production features and modifications were also carried out and it was not uncommon for Sturmgeschütz III ausf C or ausf D models to be fitted with the Topfblende mantlet and long-barrelled 7.5cm L/48 gun.

The reader should note that I have not included internal technical changes.

Notes

1. Ten firms were involved in the production of the 7.5cm gun alone, with over 100 companies contributing to the Sturmgeschütz project. Alkett was in fact a subsidiary of Rheinmetall-Borsig AG. Readers of the other books in this series will undoubtedly be familiar with these large companies.

Although this photograph was taken on the Eastern Front, it provides one of the few images of the 173 Pzkpfw III tanks that were converted to assault guns between April and July 1944. Note the very simplified commander's hatch which replaced the cupola, the armoured cover for the driver's visor and the extensive use of concrete. The much abbreviated Schürzen and the method of their attachment is similar to those commonly encountered in early 1945.

December 1942. Production of the Sturmgeschütz III ausf G begins. The superstructure side plates were set at a steeper angle than previous models and a pistol port was added to the left hull near the driver's position in place of the vision slit. An armoured shield (A), hinged at the bottom, was mounted in front of the loader's hatch to accommodate an MG 34 machine gun. These shields were also retro-fitted to many Sturmgeschütz III ausf F/8 models from early 1943.

January 1943. The fume extractor fan was relocated from the roof to the rear of the fighting compartment. A sliding armour guard was added to the roof to protect the Sfl.ZF 1a periscopic gunsight.

February 1943. Smoke candle dischargers (B) were fitted on each side of the superstructure at the front. This modification was dropped from production in the following May when it was found that enemy small arms fire was able to ignite the candles. The driver's front plate appeared without holes for the twin periscope which had been removed from production. Some vehicles had the holes plugged and welded closed.

March 1943. First production series of the Sturmhaubitze 42, based on the ausf G chassis and superstructure, was assembled by Alkett. A trial series of twelve vehicles based on rebuilds of earlier models had in fact seen service in November 1942 near Leningrad.

April 1943. Armoured skirts or Schürzen were fitted to both sides of the hull as a defence against Russian anti-tank rifles. By the following month, units in the field had been ordered to attach Schürzen to their assault guns. Many ausf F/8 models were also retro-fitted with armoured skirts.

May 1943. In place of the composite 50mm and 30mm Zusatzpanzer armour plate bolted on to the hull front (C), a single 80mm-thick plate was introduced into the manufacturing process. Due to a shortage of steel plate, this change was not fully implemented until the following November and some vehicles were fitted with the bolted-on armour until that time. The muzzle brake was fitted with side deflector flanges.

September 1943. The commander's cupola was welded into the hull roof due to a shortage of ball bearings. During the final stages of assembly, a thick paste, referred to by its commercial name of Zimmerit, was applied to all vertical armour surfaces. Prior to the vehicle being painted, the paste was applied with special tools which gave a distinctive pattern of ridges and hollows. It is fairly certain that vehicles assembled by Alkett left the plant with the so-called waffle pattern (D) and those produced by MIAG had a pattern of small squares (E). From the photographic evidence it would seem that assault guns manufactured by MAN may have had a pattern of horizontal ridges. It was not until January 1944, that units in the field were ordered to apply Zimmerit to their assault guns with, as photograph evidence shows, very mixed results. This is hardly surprising as the application was quite a complicated process (1).

October 1943. An armoured deflector was fitted in front of the cupola (F).

Notes

1. This is described in some detail in the third book in this series *Panther Tanks: German Army and Waffen-SS Normandy Campaign 1944.*

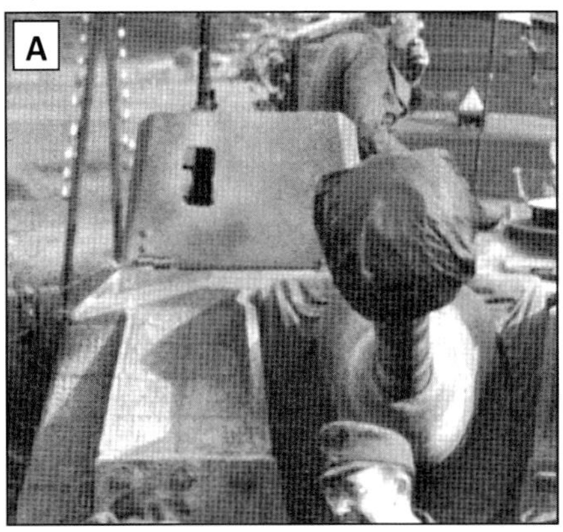
A

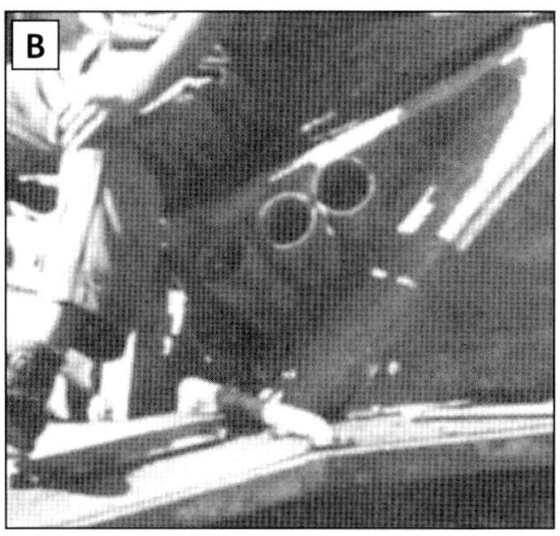
B

C

D

E

F

A

B

C

D

E

F

Notes

1. It has been suggested that the idea of using concrete originated with the Finns and that assault gun units stationed in Finland in 1944 introduced it into the German Army.

November 1943. A cast gun mantlet (A), known as a Topfblende, was introduced. This never completely replaced the earlier welded box-type which was still being installed at the end of the war and it is possible that MIAG-produced vehicles never received the Topfblende. Cast steel return rollers replaced the earlier, rubber tyre versions.

December 1943. The production of the Sturmgeschütz IV began at the Krupp's Grusonwerk plant at Magdeburg.

Early 1944. At some time early in the year, additional armour in the shape of concrete reinforcement was added to the superstructure front on either side of the main gun (B). That this was initially a field modification and not applied in the factories is fairly certain and indeed photographs exist of troops applying the concrete. Steel bars or similar were first welded to the vehicle onto which the concrete was poured and then smoothed. The concrete extended over the front plate of the superstructure and around the driver's visor and was sometimes added to the exposed side of the commander's cupola, although this practice was less common (1). Concrete was also employed, although to a very limited extent, in factory production (see April 1944 below).

March 1944. A remote-control machine gun mount (C), referred to as a Rundumsfeuer, replaced the armour shield in front of the loader's hatch. Due to a shortage of mounts, vehicles were produced for several months without the gun and a plate bolted over the hole in the roof. The loader's hatch was re-designed to open towards the sides in two halves. An improved mounting system for the hull Schürzen was introduced which allowed the plates to be fitted in combination with Ostketten extended tracks. At about this time a standardised stowage rack for the hull rear deck was introduced (D).

April 1944. Beginning in this month, and ending in July, as many as 173 obsolete Pzkpfw III tanks were converted to assault guns. These could be identified by the simplified hatch which replaced the commander's cupola, the concrete armour on either side of the main gun, the armoured hood over the driver's position and the single Bosch headlight on the left front mudguard. The loader's position was no longer protected by a shield and the machine gun was held by a raised bracket.

May 1944. A close defence weapon, or Nahverteidigungswaffe, was to have been mounted in the roof but again, due to a shortage of weapons, the installation was delayed and the resulting hole in the roof was covered by a bolted-on metal disc.

June 1944. Sockets, or Pilze, were welded to the roof of the fighting compartment allowing for the temporary mounting of a 2-ton jib boom that could be used to remove heavy parts such as the engine. A travel lock for the main gun was added to the hull front. This modification was ordered to be carried out by units in the field in the following month. A coaxial machine gun was added to the box type main gun mantlet (E).

August 1944. The rotating commander's cupola was re-introduced into production. On the Pzkpfw IV, the early style cylindrical exhaust was replaced by two Flammenvernichter (F) flame-dampening mufflers. It is probable, but far from certain, that the same modification was made to the Sturmgeschütz IV at this time. An order of 19 August directed that tanks and assault guns were to be painted in a standardised colour scheme before leaving the factory. The base colour of Dunkelgelb RAL 7028 was retained but over this large patches of Olivgrün RAL 6003 and Rotbraun RAL 8017 were to be painted. In addition, interiors would no longer be painted in Elfenbein RAL 1001 but left in the primer colour.

September 1944. The assembly firms ceased the application of Zimmerit. From September the metal Schürzen were gradually replaced in Pzkpfw IV production by panels fabricated from heavy steel mesh known as Drahtgeflechtschürzen (A), more often referred to as Thoma Schild or Thoma Schürzen. The brackets that held the panels to the hull sides were also much simplified (B).

October 1944. A coaxial machine gun (C) was added to the Topfblende gun mantlet (1). In late October or early November, the Heereswaffenamt ordered that the use of Dunkelgelb RAL 7028 as a base colour was to cease (2). Armoured vehicles would be camouflaged at the assembly plants in patches of Olivgrün and Dunkelgelb applied to the primer colour. This scheme may have been short lived.

November 1944. On 29 November a new order stipulated that armoured vehicles were to be painted in a base coat of Dunkelgrun RAL 6003 over which patches of Rotbraun 8017 and Dunkelgelb RAL 7028 were to be painted in sharp contours. This scheme was not to come into effect until 1 March 1945.

December 1944. A coupling was added to the rear hull to which rigid towing bars could be attached. This arrangement had proven more stable than towing by cable. At the same time, units in the field were ordered to make this modification to their vehicles (3). To simplify production of the Pzkpfw IV, the number of return rollers was reduced from four to three (D). This modification was carried out with the Sturmgeschütz IV although the exact date of its introduction is uncertain. On 20 December 1944 the Heereswaffenamt directed that the factory-applied camouflage scheme outlined in the November instructions was now to come into effect immediately (4).

Early 1945. At this time Sturmgeschütz III vehicles appear in photographs without the standard hull Schürzen or the brackets to hold them and it is possible that these were dropped from production in late 1944. Schürzen of various sizes, (E) and (F), held to the vehicle by a length of metal tube around which the plates were able to rotate, are also commonly seen at this time. This arrangement is often apparent on the Pzkpfw III conversions and it is entirely possible that it was later incorporated into general production. The similarities in shape, style and method of attachment evident in photographs taken on both the Eastern and Western Fronts would suggest that this was not just a field modification.

March 1945. Production of the Sturmgeschütz III ends at MIAG.

April 1945. The last Sturmgeschütz III leaves the Alkett factory in Berlin. In this month Krupp manages to assemble just three Sturmgeschütz IV before production ends.

Notes

1. Unlike the box-style mantlet, those Topfblende which had already been installed could not be re-worked to accept the co-axial machine gun.
2. The order issued to Henschel regarding the painting of the Tiger II, which has survived, was dated 31 October 1944.
3. This modification was also carried out on the Sturmgeschütz IV
4. The topic of factory-applied camouflage, and the colours and methods employed, is dealt with in some detail in *Panther Tanks: German Army and Waffen-SS, Defence of the West 1945,* the eighteenth book in this series.

A

B

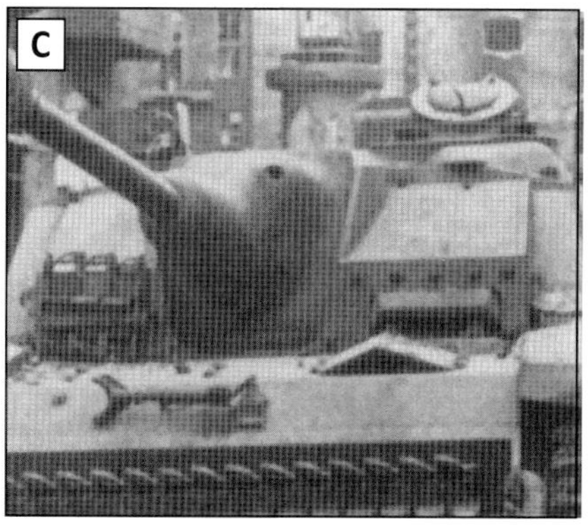
C

D

E

F

Dragon Models Ltd
B1-10/F., 603-609 Castle Peak Rd.
Kong Nam Industrial Building
Tsuen Wan, N. T., Hong Kong.
www.dragon-models.com

Tamiya Inc
Shizuoka City, Japan
www.tamiya.com

Trumpeter/Hobby Boss
NanLong Industrial Park,SanXiang,
ZhongShan,GuangDong, China
www.trumpeter-china.com
www.hobbyboss.com

Academy Plastic Models
521-1, Yonghyeon-dong, Uijeongbu-si,
Gyeonggi-do, Korea
www.academy.co.kr

Royal Model
Via E. Montale, 19-95030 Pedara, Italy
www.royalmodel.com

Italeri S.p.A.
via Pradazzo 6/b,
40012 Calderara di Reno, Bologna, Italy
www.italeri.com

Black Dog
Petr Polanka
Letecká 549, Libèice nad Vltavou
252 66, Czech Republic
www.blackdog.cz

JK Resin
Cajkovského 22
74601 Opava, Czech Republic

Hauler
Jan Sobotka,
Moravská 38, 620 00 Brno,
Czech Republic
www.hauler.cz

Voyager
Room 501, No.411 4th Village,
SPC Jinshan District, Shanghai 200540,
P.R.China
www.voyagermodel.com

Griffon Model
Suite 501, Bldg 01, 418 Middle Longpan Rd,
Nanjing, China
www.griffonmodel.com

Aber
ul. Jalowcowa 15, 40-750 Katowice, Poland
www.aber.net.pl

E.T. Model
www.etmodeller.com

Friulmodel
H 8142. Urhida, Nefelejcs u. 2., Hungary
www.friulmodel.hu

Modelkasten
Chiyoda-ku Kanda, Nishiki-Cho 1-7, Tokyo,
Japan
www.modelkasten.com
Very difficult to navigate but worthwhile.

Airfix
www.airfix.com

Revell
www.revell.com

Eduard Model Accessories
Mirova 170, 435 21 Obrnice,
Czech Republic
www.eduard.com

Master Club
www.masterclub.ru
It appears that this firm is closely associated with Armour35, a Russsian mail-order firm.

RB Model
Powstancow Wlkp.29B,
64-360 Zbaszyn,
Poland
www.rbmodel.com

M Workshop Singapore
91 Bencoolen St, Sunshine Plaza 01-58,
Singapore
www.themworkshop.com

Zvezda (Zvezda-America)
www.zvezda-usa.com
Note that the Russian catalogue is not the same as the US version.

Passion Models
www.passionmodels.jp

Kaizen
Available from Hobby Link Japan
www.hlj.com

Raupen Model
www.raupen-modell.com

Panda Plastics
www.shermantracks.com

The author would like to thank Karl Berne, Valeri Polokov and J.Howard Parker for their invaluable assistance with the photographs and period insignia and acknowledge the research of Martin Block and the late Ron Klages. Of the product manufacturers special mention should go to Roberto Reale of Royal Model, Sheng Hui of ROCHM, Jan Zdiarsky from Eduard Accessories and Freddie Leung of Dragon Models.

Photographed as it passed through Maaseik on the Dutch-Belgian frontier, this battered Sturmgeschütz III is one of the few assault guns of SS-Panzer-Regiment 10 to survive the fighting in Normandy and the retreat to the Seine. Note the unusual Mickey Mouse-style motif on the superstructure side. Although difficult to see in this print, the painting may have been repeated on the hull glacis to left of the headlight. The horseshoe was a common affectation among tank and armoured vehicle crews.